THE MODULE &
PROGRAMME
DEVELOPMENT
handbook

a practical guide to linking levels, learning outcomes & assessment

jennifer moon

**KOGAN
PAGE**

First published in 2002

Kogan Page Limited
120 Pentonville Road
London N1 9JN
UK

Stylus Publishing Inc.
22883 Quicksilver Drive
Sterling VA 20166–2012
USA

© Jennifer Moon, 2002

British Library Cataloguing in Publication Data

A CIP record for this book is available from the British Library.

ISBN 0 7494 3745 6

Typeset by Saxon Graphics Ltd, Derby
Printed and bound in Great Britain by Clays Ltd, St Ives plc

Contents

Preface

This book concerns the design and development of education. Its focus is higher education, though much of it can apply to other areas of education. Primarily the book describes the design of modules that make up programmes.

The manner and methods of viewing education in terms of the outcomes of learning rather than the curriculum content or the actions of teachers have emerged strongly in the past ten years. We can assume, after all, that it is the learning that is done by learners that is the important result in educational activity. Over recent years there has been much work that has supported the development of an 'outcome-focus'. As with many new developments in education, the work has been tortuous, with many hearts and minds to persuade, and many avenues with dead ends. Undoubtedly we are still following some dead-end avenues.

The current state of play in higher education with regard to module development reflects exactly this. We have situations in which there is a distance to go to catch up with patterns of describing programmes that are well established. At the same time, we have other situations in which, maybe, the patterns have gone into extremes in the detail of describing learning, that will prove to be unfunctional or even deleterious to higher education. This is because of the time and effort that they involve for staff and sometimes students, and because they stress the form of detail about learning that can only be realized in factual and surface approaches to learning. These things will resolve themselves in the course of time and the spreading of information, as, perhaps, we are *en route* to the next change.

The spirit of this book is the provision of information about a state of development in which we are now. In considering the linking of levels, learning outcomes and assessment criteria, the tuning of appropriate assessment methods and the work of teaching, we are in a stage of development. In this we recognize that there are probably no 'right ways' and 'wrong ways', but efforts to improve on what is present. More to the point, the book attempts to inform about present thinking and to explain the logic that underpins that thinking. The information is supported by a substantial number of examples.

About this edition

There are two versions of this handbook, this bound paperback and an A4 loose-leaf ringbound edition. This bound version is intended as a personal copy of the book, to be used by individuals as part of their own work or development. The ringbound version is intended primarily as an 'institutional' edition. Unlike this paperback, the ringbound edition is fully photocopiable and will be of particular interest to staff developers and those running short courses and workshops.

The main content of the two editions is identical, apart from the material in Chapter 10. In this edition it consists of a summary of key points. In the ringbound edition, Chapter 10 comprises photocopy masters of handouts, resources and an OHP transparency, which can be used by those working with groups, or who may need to distribute the key issues of module and programme development within their institution.

Further details of either version of *The Module and Programme Development Handbook* can be obtained from Kogan Page (see back cover for contact details).

1 Introduction: developing an outcomes basis for module development

Introduction

The introductory chapter to a book has various purposes: this chapter has three. The first purpose is to ease the reader's pathway into the subject matter. To achieve this, the chapter provides an overview of the developments that are described throughout the book: broadly what the information is, where it is and the approach taken to it. The second purpose is to set the context of the developments which are described, and this discussion is integrated with material designed to fulfil the third purpose. The third purpose is based on the premise that we construct our own knowledge and that our understandings and progression in further learning are based on that personal knowledge. On this basis, the structure of a writer's understandings is very relevant to the material that appears in a book.

The development of the ideas of programme structure

Following from the paragraph above, writing even an informative book of this sort is a personal journey plotted out across changes: in this case in higher education, new personal roles and the resultant confrontations with new ideas, conflicts and situations. If those particular new roles had not generated new problems to solve, the material of this book would either not have been written, or it would probably have looked different. The start of this book is a reflection on my passage over around nine years in the context of higher education and professional development.

This history is relatively expansive because it is more than a building of ideas. It also deals with doubts and scepticisms that have beset what can be perceived as the mechanical paperwork that necessarily accompanies the more exciting activities of teaching and processes of learning. The account represents the interweaving of several areas of concern in educational development, among which are:

■ the quality of an individual learner's experience;
■ the relationship of individual learning experiences to what we understand of the processes of teaching, learning and assessment;
■ the context of the developments – and in particular, the vision and excitement of lifelong learning developments;
■ and the need and, indeed pressure, somehow to cope with the implications of all of this in a vastly expanding field of education – with the expansion occurring very rapidly.

Threading its way through these areas of concern has been a wavering, forming and transforming philosophy of education that endeavours to account for two poles of a continuum. At one end there is personal interest in developing precision in the management of learning, and at the other end there is interest in what might be called the higher processes of higher education learning. Mixed in, too, are developing thoughts about the nature of useful knowledge and the kinds of learning that best generate that knowledge.

The real history of the book probably begins long before anything I can recollect of my own education, but in terms of my own education, the first important factor was my selection of science options at school. Science was in my family, as family members had worked in engineering and medicine. Art, music and the humanities were not. I remembering not expecting to be good at English or history or geography – and I lived up to my expectations. Interestingly I did like poetry and writing stories, but then, that was not school English: it was just what interested me at home. Interest led me astray within school learning too, as I suffered early knocks in my experiences with the examination system. I was too intrigued with the content of my learning, and not interested enough in how I needed to shape that learning in order to squeeze it effectively through GCEs (as they were then) and later A levels. I did not fail, but I did not do as well as my level of interest and thinking should have allowed. I strongly identify with more recent research on approaches to learning – I took a deep approach to learning and was not sufficiently strategic (Marton, Hounsell and Entwistle, 1997).

However, I did get to university to study zoology. It was an anatomical and descriptive version of the subject which neither particularly sparked my interest, nor furnished me with the opportunities to use my mind in the way to which it was best suited. Nor did my interest spark from the mandatory bits of chemistry in the course, which were never actually related to the zoology that we covered. They were isolated areas of learning that remained isolated. The chemistry was near physics and the zoology was very descriptive and dry, and their relationship was a theoretical one rather than a real and meaningful one at that academic level. Had I studied these subjects at a later stage, I might have been capable of making the appropriate links. In the undergraduate first year, I could not. Maybe ancillary subjects should sometimes come later in a programme, when students are better able to integrate the information – not as is usually the case, early on.

Things changed, however, in the third year of my degree. I studied the new zoological areas of ecology and animal behaviour, and they posed new hurdles of a different kind. They represented a shift from the supposed objectivity of hard science to situations of theory building and of a new kind of uncertainty. Whole rats did not always run mazes in the expected manner – certainly not with the certainty with which the muscles of frogs twitched when a specific amount of electrical current was applied to them. Nor was there any certainty as to the presence or absence of a particular species in a given habitat in which all the conditions were supposedly 'right' for that species. I had been exposed suddenly to a new structure of knowledge, which to me then, with a pure science background, seemed like a strange and disorienting new world with new rules. I can recall being totally bemused by ethological models of dripping taps. What was a model? Why play with models and not the real thing? I felt disturbed and unnerved, but had no theoretical basis on which to base a conversation about my feelings with a tutor. I do recall, however, finding the biology of the sewage works very interesting. It was nicely down to earth and comfortably real. These experiences fed into my current thinking about multidisciplinary programmes and diverse disciplinary experiences within programmes that are seen as integrated and 'single honours' (see Chapter 9).

I recall too that I remained non-strategic when it came to assessment. I was not good at keeping to the point of the question, did not revise the 'right' things, and in particular, got carried away by interesting ideas that did not accord with the interests of the lecturers who set the examination questions. I remember a night or two before finals, I became engrossed by a new-found theory of the flight of birds. Unfortunately for my results, a question on the flight of birds in the exam gave me an opportunity to expound these ideas, which did not find favour with the examiner.

At a later stage I did a Master's degree in education and began to find the kinds of learning and knowledge development that suited my mind. I left behind the sciences, and in the humanities found deliberation, reflection, argument and forms of uncertainty that felt stimulating. Maybe my level of maturity or of reflective thinking ability was significant (see Chapter 7). A time of particular stimulation and advancement in my quality of thinking was when I studied philosophy of education with a liberal-minded and excellent teacher. Because I studied it as an extra module, I did not feel that the expectations of high achievement weighed on my efforts. I wandered around the ideas that were presented, exploring my own ability to think freely about such words and ideas as learning and teaching, and the nature of education and training. It was a time when I realized that I could think effectively, that I could reach conclusions, and that they could be acceptable even if they were unconventional. They were acceptable even under examination conditions because, even though I did not 'know' much about the formal philosophies of education, I could philosophize. At that point in my education, I gained confidence in my ability to develop theory that might be new.

Another learning experience at a much later stage has fed into my thinking about the quality of learning that should be expected at Master's level. I undertook a Master's degree in health education. The student group came from a broad diversity of backgrounds. Some of the students had been working on district health promotion teams for years, and others, like me, were completely new to the subject. As happens in many Master's courses, we all studied the same programme. The programme consisted of modules that included, among other subjects, a bit of sociology, an introduction to education, and an introduction to psychology: in particular the psychology of learning, to which I will return.

Apart from the fact that I had studied these subjects in considerably greater depth before, as had others on the course, these introductory bits and pieces did not add up to anything much in the direction of health education. Nor were they much like Master's level. Little in that programme was actually challenging enough to fit into a level 2 programme. I maintained those views when, a year or so later, I was in a position of teaching and marking essays on the same programme.

Much of my subsequent university learning has been in the context of research. In research there are greater opportunities to follow up areas of interest and to make judgements in relation to the evidence and personal directions of thinking. There were what I would now perceive as difficulties in the supervision. For example, in my MEd I had my first real encounter with the topic of student learning. I studied reading for learning from texts (Moon, 1975). The subject matter was pretty incomprehensible for the social psychologist who was my tutor, and she tried to turn it towards her own interests. She failed to persuade me to follow her lead on this, and (by my judgement of the time, and also by my judgement today) gave me a very low mark. In fact I realize that I was working on material that has become very relevant in more recent times, with the wealth of research on approaches to learning (eg Marton, Hounsell and Entwistle, 1997).

In work situations, I worked variously in higher education, adult education and in health education and professional development. I was asked to look at the postgraduate health education Diplomas and Master's degrees across the UK. Coming from a long period outside higher education, I was shocked to find the apparent variations in the standard in programmes that led to the same awards. The standards were reflected in the apparent amount of contact between staff and students, the amount of assessment and the required lengths of dissertations (Moon and England, 1994).

At the same time I worked on short courses in health education (Moon, 1995a). This is where I first came across the notion of credit. These courses were often credit rated by universities, and this theoretically meant that successful participants could use the credit towards advanced standing in another higher education programme. Nurses, who were often the participants, were among the earliest professionals to use credit in this way, although in reality the importance of credit rating for most short courses was as a mark of quality rather than a key to progression.

It was my minimal expertise in the ideas of credit that enabled me to move into my next job, working for a higher education-funded unit that supported one of the major DfEE-funded credit development initiatives of the mid-1990s. The Higher Education Credit Initiative Wales (HECIW) facilitated the development and adoption of credit systems in Wales. It paralleled major projects in other parts of Britain, including the SEEC project in southern England (Southern England Credit Accumulation and Transfer Consortium). These projects followed work done by Robertson (1994) on credit accumulation and transfer systems (CATS), though in the structures that they advocated, they conflicted with the manner in which Robertson had conceived of the developments.

The credit development projects worked on the programme structures that enabled learners to earn credit for learning achieved at one institution, and use the credit towards another programme in another institution. A strong agenda for this in Wales was based on forging better links between higher and further education, in order to facilitate the widening of access to students who had previously never contemplated higher education. It was interesting to note how the existence of this agenda then seemed to alienate the more traditional universities, which are now under government and funding council pressure to widen access to their programmes.

The Welsh situation was then slightly atypical. At the time, the broader argument for credit was mainly on the basis of the portability of credit, although students have not greatly increased their mobility between institutions in these six or so years. However, many (but not all) institutions have tended to adopt the structures that support credit for other reasons. It can be a little difficult to see exactly why some of the more traditional universities did adopt the notion of credit, although certainly it allows more flexible provision and an easy movement into the principles of lifelong learning. In fact, one could say that the principles of credit accumulation and transfer are the basic underpinnings of most lifelong learning initiatives.

The main structures for credit are levels and level descriptors, learning outcomes and assessment criteria. Later chapters in this book will provide more details on the origins and evolutions of these elements of programmes from their early days in credit projects – but there is more in my personal story.

During the duration of this project, I developed a range of knowledge about programme structures and an experience of working across universities, but I also carried some scepticism. I had spent two years propounding the benefits of credit and the values of outcome-based learning described by learning outcomes. I had sat through many sessions, trying to help lecturers who had been selected to attend them to see the benefits of specifying expected learning, instead of talking about teaching and curriculum coverage. I had spent hours in meetings which were often fractious and uneasy, trying to agree the format and wordings for level descriptors with multidisciplinary teams. Later I spent many difficult days in a series of workshops at different universities, trying to help senior and staff development staff to write learning outcomes, with the idea that they would cascade this through their institutions. Endlessly I had to reassure unbelieving participants that this was not the thin end of the National Vocational Qualifications wedge – the back door, which would transform university subject matter into NVQs. Some saw the project as the advance guard of the NVQ lobby, particularly as we were funded by the DfEE.

Now, seven years later, workshops similar to these run nationally and attract large numbers of participants. Then, however, there was simply no time to stop and think about the meaning of describing programmes in this way. I felt uneasy. We were on the outside of institutions, outside teaching and learning situations, and we had no real contact with students; and yet we were telling higher education staff that they should adopt these ways of working. In one sense I liked the clarity, transparency and precision that the credit system espoused, but on the other hand I had doubts about how we were really affecting learning and the student experience of higher education.

As happens with project work so often, the project came to an end and job seeking began again. I moved into educational development at a traditional university which had been diffident about the credit developments. This gave me time to think about programme structures, teaching and learning and the experience of students. I also spent time talking with academics and even ran the odd workshop on writing learning outcomes, because like other traditional universities, this one was now recognizing the need to work in this direction.

Perhaps the main stimulant for my thinking was the process of collecting together all my formally written material, summarizing it and writing an overview as part of a PhD by portfolio.

This activity in turn led to my writing a book on reflection in learning and professional development. As I thought about this collection of material, I began to recall the sense of conflict I had felt earlier, but the nature of it was becoming clearer. I found that in talking about learning outcomes I was propounding what many considered to be a convergent and prescribed, perhaps even a narrow view of higher education. But at the same time I was writing about the higher qualities of higher education learning: reflection and broader thinking and exploration of learning. How could I be holding – or even promoting – two opposing views of higher education at the same time?

The resolution to this considerable crisis came with my realization of the importance of one thing that I had been saying for a long time: that learning outcomes should be treated as threshold statements. They should not describe the performance of the average or typical student, as so many people in workshops seemed to assume. If learning outcomes describe what a learner must do in order to pass the module, there is plenty of opportunity to promote the higher qualities of higher education learning. Chapter 5 provides more detail on this thinking.

Recognizing that I could be interested in precision and conversion in learning as well as the higher qualities of learning was a considerable relief, and helped me greatly in running workshops. I could now feel comfortable with the efforts to describe what learners must do to pass, while at the same time realizing that in describing this I was not opposing the greater development of the learner's potential. These realizations also helped me to see how the process of grading can be viewed as a means of providing an incentive for the learner to achieve more than the threshold requirements.

The story continues. I run many workshops in a new educational development post, and running workshops is an important way to learn. People ask questions which force my reasoning into new areas. In turn I have gone back to my written handouts and papers and revised them over and over again in order to encompass the reasoning, and sometimes, particularly in the last year or two, to accommodate to change and new influences. In recent times, there have been a number of changes in the formats of well used level descriptors (see Chapter 3), in the arrival of the subject benchmarking material (see Chapters 5 and 9), programme specification, and most recently in the arrival of the Quality Assurance Agency Qualifications Framework (QF) (see Chapter 3).

It is interesting to reflect on how the questions at workshops have changed over the years. The workshops on the subject matter of this book have never been easy to run. The idea that learning should be described at all can generate quite amazing angst. I would find it upsetting to realize that people saw me as anti-learning or as a hard administrator, when actually I was writing books promoting the development of more thoughtful student learning processes than many lecturers would consider. In the early days of workshops on programme structure (level descriptors and learning outcomes), as I have said above, there was much concern combined with misinformation, about NVQs and the fear that the government wanted to implement such systems to replace the traditional higher education curriculum. At the same time, there were still lecturers who would say, 'I don't want to think in advance about what I am going to teach. I will decide what to teach when I get in with the class.' The same lecturers would also say that they would decide on assessment when it came to the end of the term or semester, and that they did not need to discuss levels or standards because they would know a good or bad piece of work when they saw it.

By the late 1990s we were moving on from that line of thinking. People began to realize that focusing on the quality of learning that could and should be achieved made more sense than the old focus on teaching and curriculum. They realized that higher education was about the promoting of learning and not teaching. With the greater acceptance of learning outcomes, the part of the workshop that I then began to find difficult was the point at which I indicated that learning outcomes should be written at threshold standard. This is the new area of contention. It was hard to convince participants that learning outcomes are not written for the average or typical student, but to define those who pass and fail to pass the module. However, having reconciled my own views on the matter, I could argue with much greater confidence.

The situation now

Recently, as there has been more general acceptance of the outcomes-based approach, the questions at workshops have focused more on the technicalities of using learning outcomes and level descriptors, and on their role in assessment. People will ask about how many learning outcomes must be passed in a module (see Chapter 5), and what sort of assessment criteria to write (see Chapter 6). I find myself more and more needing to explain that describing learning in terms of level descriptors or learning outcomes is a form of word-play; that describing learning is a slippery occupation, and that words skid around in their meanings. We are doing our best to be clearer about something that has been very unclear. We have not arrived at a point where learning can be described with great precision, nor are we ever likely to get there, but we are doing our best to improve, and improvement is a process and not an end-point.

It is also important to stress that there are no right answers to describing learning or to describing the structure of programmes. The elements of programme structure and the manner in which they are linked that are discussed in this book are not 'right', but are those that are largely in use at the present. They are accompanied by justifications which seem appropriately to match current views of teaching and learning. However, they can be superseded. We can probably still do better. Because improvement is a process, we can openly admit that some parts of the process are still undergoing development.

Level descriptors and learning outcomes are now in use relatively commonly, and use itself has led to modification and improvement. However, there seem still to be weak links in some aspects of programme structure, mainly those that concern assessment criteria and their expression in assessment tasks. As I explain in Chapter 6, there is still much misunderstanding about what constitutes an assessment criterion, and the ways in which such criteria can be used. Further thinking about assessment criteria inevitably brings one to another difficult issue: how specific should we be in telling students what they need to do in order to pass or get a particular grade in an assessment task? There can be no blanket answer to questions like this. Decisions as to the specificity of descriptions of learning, beyond a certain level of clarity, should rightly be a joint concern of those who are experts in that area of knowledge and educationists who understand the educational issues. Ideally at least these understandings would be present in one person who can explain and guide others.

Modification in patterns of programme structure is not just a matter of further tuning of what is there already. Modification is also a response to new influences. A little over a year ago, for example, a talk about levels and level descriptors was simple. There were few options and few matters for choice. Now in a workshop there is much more to explain, and more choice to be made about what set of descriptors to use for what purpose. One influence has been the arrival of the Qualifications Framework, with its set of associated qualification descriptors. In addition, there have been changes agreed in the most widely used credit consortium descriptors: the SEEC descriptors (see Chapter 3).

The influences that affect level descriptors are specific. There are other influences which affect modules, programmes and the pattern of provision of institutions in more general terms. Examples of these are the initiatives that encourage the learning of skills by students; the practical developments that can be placed under the umbrella term of lifelong learning; deliberations about the nature of multidisciplinary programmes (see Chapter 9); the development of foundation degrees; the actual and expected changes in the external review of provision by the Quality Assurance Agency (QAA); and the influence of student fees.

The advent of the charging of student fees is a pervasive, but powerful influence. Its influence is not only negative. It certainly presses higher education into more meticulous administrative procedures, but it also makes it more reasonable for students to expect an appropriate experience in higher education, and therefore forces greater accountability. It is one of the factors that drive the development of greater transparency in the processes of assessment. Teaching staff are required to be more clear about the assessment criteria on which they have based judgements of pass and fail or grading.

Student fees and the general financial situation of students influence higher education in other ways that may be relevant to this book. Most students do part-time work. This tends to mean that many are actually part-time students. Having less time and energy for study puts pressure on students to become more strategic, more often learning only what they have to learn – and guided by their expectations of assessment in their choices about what modules to study. These factors raise a number of issues about the clarity of provision and the transparency of processes of assessment.

Some institutions capitalize on students' part-time work as a source for learning employability and other learning skills in setting up work experience modules (Watton, Collings and Moon, 2002 – in preparation). Typically in these modules, students undertake various tasks that facilitate their learning from their part-time work. Such modules are unique, and they have demanded and continue to demand considerable thought about how to make best use of them and of their outcomes alongside conventional learning – and in particular, how to describe them in terms of levels and learning outcomes.

General introduction to the book

The section above will have indicated that this book represents a pulling-together of much material. There are plenty of publications on which it is based, but the ideas have often not been focused in one place. It could be said that the common idea in the book is the development of programmes – indeed the title reflects this – but in fact most of the book is about the development of modules that make up programmes, recognizing the need for linked and logical thinking in programme development. We think about logical structure in what we teach. We have always done that. In the past we have considered considerably less what students learn or how they are to be assessed. We may also see procedures such as programme evaluation and quality assessment as distant and distinct from the real act of teaching – or is it the real act of learning that is relevant here?

Is it learning or teaching that we are dealing with here? The book actually deals with the development of what might be best termed 'blocks of learning'. Words such as 'programme', 'course', and particularly 'curriculum development' or 'design' tend to imply a block of teaching. A characteristic of the new ways of looking at higher education is that it focuses on the learning that results from the programme, and generally not on the teaching element implied by 'programme'. However there is a shortage of specific terminology, and with the proviso that the focus is mainly on learning and not on teaching, in this book the term 'programme' is used to describe the processes that lead to a qualification in higher education. A programme is usually made up of modules, although sometimes the word 'unit' is used to mean something similar. The word 'module' is more learning-orientated, since it seems to be acceptable to include a module that has no teaching content, with perhaps a learning contract to provide the orientation. Sometimes in the book the term 'course' is used to mean something like a short programme, but complete in itself and without a modular structure.

The primary intention of this book is to provide a straightforward and systematic guide to the process of developing modules, and as a consequence programmes, and to the manner of use of the various elements in the process. Among the elements are levels, level descriptors, learning outcomes, aims and objectives, assessment criteria, assessment methods and associated teaching strategies. These elements of module or course development are drawn together in a 'map of module or course development' that is described in the next chapter. Not only does this map describe the basic links between the elements of a block of learning, but it also provides a logical sequence for the chapters in the book.

The last but one chapter is about programmes themselves. Though it addresses the new requirements for the writing of programme specification, and also issues in multidisciplinary programmes, the chapter considers the way in which modules relate to programmes.

The last chapter actually adds nothing new to the book. It represents a collection of the main ideas expressed in the previous chapters. The points are indexed into the chapters so that the chapter can act as an elaborated summary of the important points. It also provides a resource to support staff development around the topics covered here.

Some notes on the use of words

Some of the words used, and the ways in which they are used, need to be introduced at this point.

- The words 'student' and 'learner' are used interchangeably.
- The gender of a subject is always a difficult issue. Among the options are to use the male gender throughout, with the conventional assumption that this includes the female; to use the cumbersome or unsayable 'he or she' or 's/he' or to pluralize the gender; or to use 'they' as a false singular. The latter is grammatically incorrect. As I have done in my other books, I use the

feminine gender throughout this book. It is 100 per cent correct at least 50 per cent of the time.

■ Another word issue that is relevant in several places in this book is the clear separation of the activities of 'teaching' and 'learning'. Teaching and learning are different activities undertaken at a given time by different actors in the educational situation – and yet there is confusion or 'fudging' of the words with the use of the terms 'learning and teaching' very frequently. It is particularly important to be clear about what is teaching and what is learning in the context of this book.

■ To help with the inevitable sets of letters and acronyms that beset higher education and society in general, there is a glossary at the end of the book (page 188).

2 A map of module development

Introduction

This short chapter introduces a basic map with two purposes. It is a map of module development, and the sequence of it provides a logical sequence for discussion of the elements of module development within the first part of this book. While these few pages scarcely constitute a chapter, presenting the map here allows us to head the subsequent chapters with titles that indicate exactly the nature of their content.

The map of module or course development is shown in Figure 2.1. The map applies to the structures of modules and of short courses, or to any block of learning that has a set of learning outcomes that are assessed at the end of the block. That will often not apply to a whole programme defined as in Chapter 1. It can apply to modules as they are usually defined in higher education, or it could apply to a course.

In following the sequence of the model, we will be making a distinction between the processes of the basic development of the module (from now on, letting 'module' account for 'course' as well) and grading. The implication of this is that the map is concerned with student achievement at threshold, and for the moment it does not take account of the addition of a grading system above the threshold. It is simpler to view grading as a process that is added on to basic development.

In reality, the actual sequence of the map may rarely be followed in the design process of a module, as there is a tendency to start with curriculum, staff experiences or interests, and practical issues such as the availability of the particular expertise. The map can be considered an ideal sequence, and as such it provides a rationale for the links between level, learning outcomes, assessment criteria, assessment and teaching methodologies. It has a particularly important role as a tool for checking the whole design for consistency once the initial development is completed.

The figure of the map is repeated in each of the subsequent chapters in this book when an element of module development is

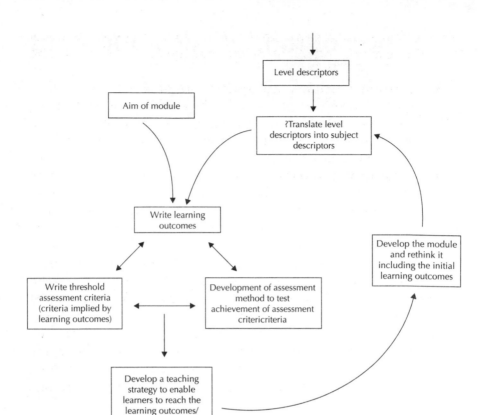

Figure 2.1 Basic map of module development

more comprehensively introduced. Now, however, we briefly introduce the terms and the sequence that links them.

- **Level descriptors** are descriptions of what a learner is expected to achieve at the end of a level of study. Levels are hierarchical stages that represent increasingly challenging learning to a learner. The term 'level' is now used instead of 'years of study', since a student on a part-time programme may study for six years to reach the same qualification as that achieved by another full-time student in three years (see Chapters 3 and 4).
- **Aims** indicate the general direction or orientation of a module, in terms of its content and sometimes its context

within a programme. An aim tends to be written in terms of the teaching intentions or the management of the learning (see Chapter 5)

■ **Learning outcomes** are statements of what a learner is expected to know, understand or be able to do at the end of a module and of how that learning will be demonstrated. Unlike aims, they are couched in terms of what the learner is expected to learn (see Chapter 5).

■ **Assessment criteria** are statements that indicate, in a more detailed manner than the learning outcome, the quality of performance that will show that the learner has reached a particular standard that is reflected in the learning outcome (see Chapters 6 and 8).

■ The **assessment method** is often confused with assessment criteria. It is the task that is undertaken by learners that is the subject of assessment. It provides the context for assessment criteria (see Chapters 7 and 8).

■ A **teaching strategy**, in terms of this map, is the support that needs to be given to learners to enable them to achieve the learning outcomes. Learning can, of course, be achieved without the involvement of teaching (see Chapters 7 and 8).

Level descriptors and module aims guide the writing of learning outcomes. A set of level descriptors may act directly as a guide for the writing of learning outcomes, or the level descriptors may be translated into descriptors for the discipline or programme. In either case, the level descriptors ensure that the outcome statement is clearly related to a particular level, and they provide an indication of agreed achievements. Learning outcomes are derived from consideration of level descriptors and aims. Learners must show that they can achieve the learning outcomes to gain credit for the module. Aims provide a rationale or a direction for the module.

Learning outcomes imply the assessment criteria. Assessment criteria may be developed from the learning outcome or from the assessment method or task, but in either case they should relate to the learning outcome. There are many reasons for developing assessment tasks, and these will affect the manner in which an assessment task is designed. However, the central purpose of the task with which we are concerned is to test that the learning outcomes have been achieved. A teaching strategy, on this model, is seen as being designed in relation to assessment processes, providing the support necessary to enable the students to be successful in attaining the threshold indicated in assessment criteria. We also acknowledge the importance of the interrelationship between assessment methods and teaching strategies in covering both topics in the same chapter.

The map is not just for development processes. It also guides the programme developer in checking on the coherence and consistency of the elements within the programme. This means going through it perhaps several times, ensuring that each part that is linked to another part by lines is clearly linked in terms of the structure of the module. Perhaps the most significant linkage is that between learning outcomes and assessment criteria.

Any element in the cycle of development can be changed, except the agreed level descriptors which are fixed.

3 Levels and level descriptors

Introduction

In a recent survey of higher education institutions in England, Wales and Northern Ireland, 76 per cent of the 92 HEIs that responded claimed to be using level descriptors (Johnson and Walsh, 2000). Sets of level descriptors are used at many points in the development of higher educational provision. They are used to match whole programmes to national expectations in the National Qualifications Framework (see below), to compare provision within an institution, to compare modules within a programme, and at the stage of writing appropriate learning outcomes for modules. As well as being discussed in this chapter, these and other uses of level descriptors are explored in Chapter 4.

The major initial work on detailed level descriptors in the UK originated in two Department of Education and Employment credit development projects in the early to mid-1990s. The projects involved many higher education institutions in the south of England that were members of the SEEC consortium, and all of the Welsh institutions (HECIW). Between the two projects, around 50 higher education institutions were represented. In these initial developments, level descriptors provided a structure for the use of credit in higher education. Other forms of level descriptors have been produced in recent years, many of them based on the original SEEC/HECIW descriptors.

In 2001 the Quality Assurance Agency (QAA) issued the Qualifications Framework (QAA, 2001a). The Framework describes the level of qualifications that are offered in higher education and therefore represents another set of descriptors. The latter, however, are qualification descriptors, describing the expected outcomes of those achieving particular qualifications at the specified levels. Apart from the conceptual difference, these QAA descriptors are brief and may be less useful than the more detailed SEEC descriptors for some of the applications of level descriptors that are described later. For example, because of their relative brevity, they would not provide the same degree of guidance for the writing of learning outcomes. The

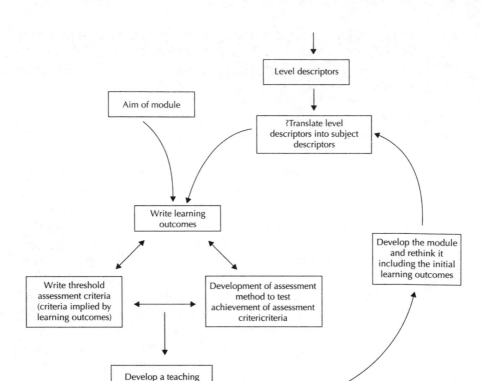

Figure 3.1   Basic map of module development

Quality Assurance Agency indicated that the sets of level descriptors developed by other agencies are acceptable to reviewers in the process of programme review (QAA, 2000a).

This chapter takes a broad view of levels and level descriptors, considering their origins and the differences between the various types of descriptors that are available. As was indicated in Chapter 2, I repeat the basic map in order to maintain a view of the sequence of discussion used in this book. The role of levels is to provide a structure for educational provision, and the role of the descriptors is to provide an agreed and relatively standardized statement of what learners are expected to achieve at each level.

Examples of several sets of level descriptors are given in the Appendices. The text of this chapter provides information about the bases on which these were designed, and the purposes for which they are intended. (See Appendix 1, SEEC level descriptors, and Appendix 2, Quality Assurance Agency Qualifications Framework qualification descriptors.)

The background to levels in higher education

The structure of a programme in higher education used to be described in terms of years: thus we would talk of a student in her first, second or third (or perhaps fourth) year of an undergraduate programme. Generally the reference to a year of study conveyed the complexity of teaching, and the demands of learning and assessment that the learner experienced, so that the level of both was higher in year 3 than in year 1, for example. While the patterns of higher education were in their traditional form, this system was adequate. For example, there were relatively few students – well under 10 percent of the relevant population age group – and nearly all were full time. Those students did not tend to change programmes, and teaching and learning were meant to be integrated and not modular (see Chapter 1).

Under these circumstances, there was an assumption that everyone agreed what a second year student's work looked like. The assumption was probably reasonable. When the matter of expectations of student achievement was in dispute, there was reliance on the interactions between teaching staff and external examiners to sort it out. How new lecturers 'absorbed' expectations of student achievement was an interesting issue – and it still is.

Evidence of this approach to levels is demonstrated in the Council for National Academic Awards *Handbook* (CNAA, 1991), in which level 2 achievement is described simply as 'Work equivalent to the standard required for the fulfilment of the general aims of the second year of a full-time degree'. Such a self-referenced approach does not facilitate the maintenance of an agreed concept of standards.

In recent years many things have changed. Student numbers have risen and there are more staff and fewer opportunities for them to discuss expectations of student work. Particularly important in the development of levels was a series of changes that could be associated with the development of credit accumulation and transfer systems (CATS). This system implied that learning should be made more 'portable', so that a learner could gain credit for learning that had been achieved, and potentially use that credit as part of an award in another institution or another situation.

Partly as a result of the orientation of higher education towards a credit system, many programmes were redeveloped into a series of modules ('modularization'). A modularized and credit-based system, along with the political pressures to widen access to higher education and to view it in the context of lifelong learning, brought about an increase in part-time study and developments associated with the accreditation of short courses such as those in professional development. Further developments that make higher education more flexible and better adapted to the needs of a modern economy are the adoption of methods of accrediting learning that has resulted from prior experience (APEL/APL) and learning in work-based situations ('work-based learning').

These changes required a move away from the traditional description of learning in terms of the year of study in an under-graduate programme to a system that could be applied more widely. The existence of part-time programmes meant that the demands of learning could no longer be described realistically in terms of the year, as a student might be taking six years to reach an honours degree. Similarly APEL and the accreditation of work-based learning or short courses have made it important to be able to recognize where a body of learning 'fits' into the patterns of insti-tution-based higher education. The 'fit' will relate to the content of the learning and its level. These ideas are expressed as learning outcomes associated with a specific level.

We may have moved away from talking of the complexity of study in terms of the year of study. However we have generally retained the notion that in England and Wales there are three years of study in most undergraduate programmes towards a Bachelor's honours degree. This has been the principal undergraduate provision in England, Wales and Northern Ireland. Thus in these countries, most systems of levels utilize three levels of under-graduate education which lead to an honours degree, and this will still apply even if there are, in total, four years (or more) of under-graduate study. In Scotland many undergraduate programmes take four years to reach honours degree level, and in order to take account of this different tradition, four undergraduate Scottish levels are usually present in level descriptors.

In terms of postgraduate education, different patterns of levels have been used in different systems. Until recently, the level descriptors in most general use relied on one level for all post-graduate provision (often called 'level M'). This level applied mainly to Master's programmes. However, with the increase in taught doctorates, it became important to recognize that Master's degrees did not represent the highest level of learning, and current descriptors now tend to split postgraduate provision into Master's and taught doctorate levels. Because most systems of level descriptors are concerned with learning that has been prescribed in a teaching/learning situation, level descriptors tend not to refer to research degrees (for example, PhDs). The QAA descriptors, however, are qualification descriptors and therefore do relate to research programmes (see below). It is the endpoint of the qualification that is at issue.

Levels are generally arranged in a hierarchy, so that a higher level is seen as more complex in terms of learning than a lower level, and there is an assumption that levels higher in the hierarchy subsume the learning from lower levels. Thus someone entering a programme at Master's level would be expected to have attained learning described below Master's level. She would be expected to have attained an honours degree, or to demonstrate the achievement of learning equivalent to that standard. Generally numerical labels have been used for levels, but the new system of levels in the QAA Qualifications Framework introduces a series of letters. These are still arranged in a hierarchy (see below). To confuse matters there are several systems of numbering of levels in operation at present, as will also be seen below. While some systems relate numbering only to higher education, starting at level 1 for the first level of undergraduate education, others take into account previous learning (eg post-16 or lower). Table 3.1 (page 33) demonstrates some of the different systems in operation.

In terms of definition, a level is an indication of the standard of difficulty of the work that a student will need to be able to undertake in order to be deemed to have achieved the credit for the learning. One formal definition is the following:

> A level is an indicator of relative demand; complexity; depth of study and learner autonomy.
>
> (Gosling and Moon, 2001)

In the case of the QAA qualification descriptors, the levels relate to the standard of difficulty of the work that the learner will have demonstrated in order to gain the qualification. This is somewhat difficult conceptually, particularly when there are several qualifications at a level. For example at the second higher education level (intermediate level) there are foundation degrees, higher national diplomas, undergraduate diplomas in higher education and ordinary degrees.

The new development of foundation degrees exemplifies the further and productive exploitation of the use of credit and levels in the building of degrees. The degrees represent a qualification at the second level of the Qualifications Framework. Not only is accredited work experience included in all foundation degrees, but also the credit that students require to achieve the qualification is allocated in different ways in different models that are offered.

Level descriptors

The achievement of learning to be expected at each different level in a system is spelled out in level descriptors. A definition of level descriptors indicates that:

> level descriptors are generic statements describing the characteristics and context of learning expected at each level against which learning outcomes and assessment criteria can be reviewed in order to develop modules and assign credit at the appropriate level.
>
> (Gosling and Moon, 2001)

There is no one agreed manner in which to describe learning, so in different sets of descriptors, different specific aspects of learning tend to be described. Sometimes this is because there is emphasis on different forms of learning. For example, in the level descriptors used by the University for Industry, there is more concern for the learning relevant to work places (Jackson, 1999). Most descriptors, however, focus on some or all of the following:

- complexity of knowledge and understanding;
- standard of cognitive skills such as analysis, synthesis and so on;
- other skills, variably termed key or transferable skills;
- and some distinguish more practical skills (eg using information technology).

Sometimes there is a statement about the level of responsibility that a learner at a particular level might take in a work or professional situation, or in terms of personal management. Often embedded among the descriptors there will also be a reference to the autonomy of the learner as a learner and/or the amount of guidance required for the learner as a learner. We add these, therefore to the list:

- the expected responsibility of the learner;
- the autonomy or independence of the learner;
- guidance required by the learner.

The relative standard of level descriptors

A characteristic that represents another variation between the different sets of level descriptors is the standard of student learning within any level to which they refer. While the descriptors given as examples in this book (see Appendices 1 and 2) describe learning that has been achieved at a level in higher education, the description might be cast at different standards within the level. It could be cast in terms of aspiration (what it is hoped the brightest students will achieve); in terms of the expectation of the typical student; or it could indicate what students must achieve in order to have reached the standard implied by the level. While this difference may appear to be fundamental, the reality is that such precision of wording to describe any form of learning is very difficult to achieve for generic descriptors. It becomes easier if level descriptors are translated into the discourse of discipline or programme or module.

Given the difficulty of attaining the precision to describe levels at threshold, the SEEC descriptors are described as providing 'guidance' as to expected achievement. In terms of relating level descriptors to standards, this system is appropriate so long as learning outcomes, which relate modules to level descriptors, are written at threshold, or in terms of what the learners must do to pass the module.

The types of level descriptors, and some examples

We have indicated earlier not only that there are different sets of level descriptors in use in the UK, but also that they differ conceptually.

In presenting some examples of sets of level descriptors, this section also addresses the distinction between the two main types of descriptors: credit level descriptors and qualification descriptors.

Credit level descriptors

Detailed generic level descriptors that have been designed for use in more than one institution have been available for around six years in Britain, originating in the work of the credit development projects of the mid-1990s. The main initiative at that time resulted in a set of descriptors developed jointly between two DfEE-funded credit development projects, SEEC and HECIW. The development process involved background research on descriptors that had already been developed elsewhere, in particular, New Zealand (Methven, 1994). Work on other courses was particularly helpful too (eg Richards, 1992; NHSTD, 1994; Bement and Lyons, 1994). There was also a consideration of Bloom's taxonomy of educational objectives (Bloom, 1956) and similar tools. These resources generally provided ideas for appropriate vocabulary for the description of cognitive skills. Bloom, for example, brought into wide use such words as 'synthesis', 'analysis' and 'evaluation'.

In the project work there were also many meetings of academics from different disciplines from the member institutions. An example of the tasks of the meetings is to seek to agree a common set of words for the process of analysis as undertaken by students in any discipline, at the different levels in undergraduate and the (then) one level of postgraduate education. This is an interesting task when diverse groups of academics such as medical educators, English and mathematics lecturers are attempting to agree words that describe their understanding of (say) analysis within the context of their disciplines. Considerable learning took place within the meetings, apart from the seeking of the intended outcomes of level descriptors. The process took several months and the descriptors were approved in 1996 after final consultations within the separate projects (Moon, 1995b; SEEC, 1996; HECIW, 1996).

It is important to recognize that there were dissenting voices in the process. There were some who felt that it is not possible to use a common vocabulary for all disciplines. Others felt that the generic descriptors that resulted from the development work represented 'all things to all people', and lost the essential complexities of student learning (eg Winter, 1993; Winter, 1994; Winter, 1994a). There is good reason for sympathy with such views, but as we have suggested before, in a world in which communication between teachers is increasingly difficult, where student numbers are high and in which demands for transparency are growing, we have improved our ability to describe and account for learning. There may yet be much learning to do or even new systems of describing learning to embrace.

The SEEC/HECIW descriptors were launched in 1996 (SEEC, 1996; HECIW, 1996) with associated guidelines, the spirit of which is included in the text of the chapters on level descriptors. They used three undergraduate higher education levels, and at postgraduate stage they worked at that time with one level (level M). Subsequently both consortia have adopted two postgraduate levels (Master's and taught doctorate).

In 2000, SEEC consulted its member institutions on the adoption of a new version of the level descriptors that had been developed by Anglia Polytechnic University (APU). These descriptors used most of the wording of the original SEEC/HECIW descriptors, but redeveloped them in a new format both for easier use and to accord with headings suggested in the Dearing Report (NCIHE, 1997). These headings emphasized the skills element in higher education learning. There were also minor word changes to bring greater accord with the vocabulary of the QAA qualification descriptors. Further modifications have produced a more usable labelling system within the descriptors, so that the increasing sophistication of learning can be followed clearly through the different levels. It is important to recognize progression in the standard of learning through the levels. There was agreement to adopt the revised descriptors (which are the version shown in Appendix 1).

Later processes of development of level descriptors had the advantage of being able to refer to the successes and failures of earlier efforts. Thus the original SEEC/HECIW descriptors have contributed to most subsequent developments in the UK, including the Qualifications Framework descriptors.

The Northern Ireland Credit Accumulation and Transfer System (NICATS) descriptors also made use of the SEEC/HECIW descriptors in their development. Usefully, the NICATS descriptors were developed in two versions: a brief version and a more detailed version (NICATS, 1998). These acknowledged the different uses of descriptors, for example in administration and in educational and staff development. It was also considered to be useful that the NICATS descriptors used nine levels which started with post-16 provision as level 1. The incorporation of levels below higher education levels facilitates the development of a 'seamless' educational progression from below further education entry (entry level), through further education levels (1–3), then into five higher education levels (three undergraduate levels and two postgraduate levels). It was for this reason that the brief descriptors from Northern Ireland were adopted in a later DfEE project, when the several credit development agencies across the UK were working towards the development of a common UK credit framework (InCCA, 1998).

A set of somewhat different general descriptors was developed by the Qualifications and Curriculum Agency (QCA, www) to provide general descriptions for National Vocational Qualifications levels. These are sometimes used in higher education for vocational subject areas. They start prior to GCSE level and progress to level 5. Levels 4 and 5 are generally agreed to be relevant to higher education, representing the competence achieved in undergraduate and postgraduate levels respectively.

As indicated earlier The University for Industry has also developed a set of level descriptors (Jackson, 1999). Similarly to the NICATS descriptors, these run from entry level through levels 1 to 8, with levels 4 to 8 (inclusive) representing the higher education levels. Unlike the other descriptors, these have been designed specifically for use of learners in the context of work. The descriptors relate to the kind of learning relevant to work situations (eg including descriptors of complexity and responsibility of the subject matter, and innovation and originality in the approach of learners).

We have suggested that it is appropriate to term the descriptors above as credit level descriptors for reasons that will be explained below. We now come to consideration of the QAA qualification descriptors, which differ conceptually from the credit level descriptors, although in practice they may well be used in many similar ways and for similar purposes to the credit level descriptors.

QAA National Qualifications Framework qualification descriptors

For some time, the QAA has been working on the presentation of a Qualifications Framework. A qualification framework was required in order to make sense of the variety of higher education awards available at different levels – and to reduce the disparity between some of them in different institutions. In particular it was felt that the provision of higher education was no longer comprehensible to employers. From a survey reported in the NQF paper, there was evidence that employers taking on those with higher education qualifications often did not understand what had been studied and the meaning of the qualification that had been attained.

The final version of the Qualifications Framework for England, Wales and Northern Ireland was made available early in 2001 (QAA, 2001a). In order to locate the qualifications described at in higher education, the framework presents a set of qualification descriptors and a brief indication of what the typical student should be able to do as a result of working to that level. While the QAA has indicated that subject reviewers should be content for institutions to continue to use the descriptors already in use (QAA, 2000b), there is some confusion as to the role of the new descriptors and how they relate to the credit descriptors already in use.

The QAA qualification descriptors 'exemplify the outcomes of the main qualification at each level and demonstrate the nature of change between levels'(QAA, 2001a: 5). The descriptors are presented in two parts at each level. The first part is worded as 'a statement of outcomes, achievement of which a student should be able to demonstrate for the award of the qualification' (p 5). This implies that the standard of these descriptors is at threshold. The second part is a statement of 'the wider abilities that the typical student should be expected to have developed' (p 5), and the reference to the 'typical student' suggests that this part of the descriptors is designed to act more like a guide to standards, as do the SEEC credit level descriptors.

The first part of the qualification descriptors is intended for an audience of those who design, approve and review academic programmes, and the second part is for a wider audience of those not directly associated with higher education, such as employers.

The conceptual difference between credit level descriptors and qualification descriptors

While there is a conceptual difference in intended uses for these two sets of descriptors, it is likely that many practitioners will not recognize the distinction in theory or practice. The SEEC credit descriptors provide guidance as to what a learner is expected to achieve at the end of a level in higher education. In this context 'level' is defined in accordance with the usual credit volume for a year equivalent of study. For undergraduates this is 120 credits, and for postgraduates the volume is 180 credits. The difference between the numbers of undergraduate and postgraduate credits is explained by the notion that postgraduates undergo a longer period of study in a year than do undergraduates.

There is a tendency to assume in the SEEC descriptors that the level of study is largely made up of modules that are at that identified level. Such an assumption becomes a little difficult in some of the new qualifications, where the final 'level' of the award may be made up of modules of different levels (see below). For this reason, the qualification descriptors might not be seen to be appropriate to use for consideration of the level of modules or units, but equally, credit descriptors do tend to assume that a level implies that most study is at that level (Moon, 2001a).

There is, therefore, a different theoretical basis for the QF qualification descriptors and the several versions of credit descriptors, and the different bases are particularly evident when qualifications may be made up of modules from different (credit) levels at the stage of the award (see earlier). For example, the ordinary degree is at level I (intermediate level) in the qualifications framework, but may contain a substantial volume of credits at level 3. In many institutions a successful learner may have had to achieve a number of credits at level 3. Institutions will need to consider what to do about the ordinary degree in terms of its level and credit make-up, since it has been a useful 'fall-back' position for students who do not properly complete an honours degree at level H.

In a converse situation, the learner on a Master's programme in some institutions may have achieved some of the 180 credits for the award at level 3. In both cases, the Qualifications Framework theoretically takes account of the make-up of the qualification by making no actual reference to credit and talking only in terms of the outcome of the qualification, however it is achieved. There has been considerable concern about the apparent 'unhitching' of credit from qualifications, because it is felt that a few words about an outcome of a qualification do not provide sufficient quality assurance for the standard of the qualification. Conventions about the credit structure of a qualification act as much greater assurance that the learner has, in total, studied for sufficient time and at sufficiently high levels to have achieved the qualification.*

Another issue that is clarified by using some reference to credit in qualifications descriptors is characterizing the differences between the several qualifications that can terminate at a particular level in the framework. It is difficult to see how the statement that the QAA descriptors 'exemplify the outcomes of the main qualification at each level' (QAA, 2001a: 5), can coexist with that describing 'outcomes that cover the great majority of existing qualifications'. This confusion exists particularly at the second – or the intermediate – level, which is, as we have seen, the awarding level for a range of qualifications that will require to be seen as substantially different in order to continue in coexistence in a meaningful manner. QAA appears to recognize this anomaly in the suggestion that benchmark statements may be developed to provide 'additional qualification descriptors'.

'Additional qualification descriptors' may be exemplified in the case of the new intermediate level foundation degree. This degree is characterized by its direct and overt relevance to a vocation (eg Art and Design or Tourism), by the inclusion of associated work experience and by the (essential) identification of progression routes beyond the foundation degree to an honours degree by further study of modules at level 3. Interestingly, though the end-point of the foundation degree is a qualification at intermediate level, it may be made up of different patterns of credit structures.

We indicate in this section that in terms of actual level implied by descriptors, there are some apparent differences between the SEEC credit descriptors and the QAA qualification descriptors. Because it is possible that the two sets of descriptors may be used together, some notes on a comparison between the two sets of levels are included in Appendix 3.

---

* Since this book was first written, the credit consortia of England, Wales and Northern Ireland have developed credit guidelines to support the National Qualifications Framework.

In summary

It is perhaps ironic that the various attempts to produce agreements about the various structures in higher education learning over the last eight or so years have resulted in a current state that is diverse rather than unified. This partly demonstrates the efforts on the part of higher education to respond to initiatives and agendas such as widening access and lifelong learning. Aspects of the diversity do support what is meant to be a more diverse higher education; however, in some ways the diversity is apt to produce confusion where the attempt was to simplify. Table 3.1 is an attempt to provide an indication of various systems of level descriptors, showing the different terms used for 'level', the different numbers of levels utilized and an approximate comparison. Most of the systems have not undergone formal comparison. (Note: there is no specific agreement about these equivalences – they are represented as an indication only.)

Where we make reference to levels in the subsequent text, we will adopt the system of the SEEC credit level descriptors: levels 1, 2, 3, Master's and taught doctorate.

Theoretical and practical issues in the use of level descriptors

Theoretical issues

Dividing the issues in the use of level descriptors into those of a theoretical and those of a practical nature is a matter of convenience and organization. Level descriptors are only of interest for their practical meaning for the functioning of higher education, and hence the theory is only of interest for its practical implications.

The use of level descriptors along with learning outcomes puts the focus on learning

The fact, for example, that level descriptors are described in terms of learning represents a subtle, but highly significant change in the view of higher education. No longer is the focus on a concern with the complexity of input (teaching), but it is on the complexity of output: what the student can do as a result of study at a particular

Table 3.1 A comparison of some different systems of level descriptors in the UK. The table makes broad generalizations and represents no specific agreements about equivalence

Levels	SEEC	QAA QF	NICATS InCCA	QCA	Wales	Scotland* SHE SCQF
Pre-higher education (HE)	n/a	n/a	Entry level plus levels 1–3	levels 1–3	n/a	n/a Levels 1–6
First HE level	Level 1	Level C	Level 4		Level 1	SHE1 Level 7
Second HE level	Level 2	Level I	Level 5	Level 4	Level 2	SHE2 Level 8
Third HE level	Level 3	Level H	Level 6		Level 3	SHE3 Level 9
						SHE4 Level 10
First postgraduate level	Master's level	Level M	Level 7	Level 5	Master's level	Master's
Second postgraduate level	Taught doctorate level	Level D	Level 8		Taught doctorate level	Doctorate

* SHE = Scottish Higher Education level; SCQF = Scottish Credit and Qualifications Framework (QAA, 2001b)

level. This represents a recognition that teaching and learning are different – if usually linked – activities. It recognizes that talking only of the curriculum or the teaching that a student is expected to have experienced is not a reliable measure of standards achieved in general or in terms of the individual student. Much of the earlier educational writing considers the improvement of learning by putting the focus on instruction techniques or the environment of learning, but not on the learning activities of the learner herself (Moon, 2001b).

The use of a system of level descriptors creates transparency in higher education

Along with learning outcomes (see Chapter 5), the use of level descriptors helps to make higher education practice more explicit and more transparent. The actual precision in the thinking is not necessarily new, and the work on elucidating level descriptors may have often have done no more than to put on paper the sorts of idea that were always in the minds of the more concerned teachers. Anyone who has ever engaged in the kind of conversation that compared the work of one year group of students with that of another has thought in terms of levels and the related expectations of achievement. However, expression of them now on paper allows discussion of them, disagreement, agreement or modification as necessary.

What does become apparent in putting level descriptors on paper, however, is the sheer difficulty of making words describe the subtlety of our expectations of student work. There is still the 'I know good work when I see it' feeling around. Words are blunt instruments, and the construction of level descriptors is a matter of doing the best possible job in describing the outcomes of the learning process. The concept of learning is slippery, complex and multidimensional. Similarly, words that we use to describe learning can be equally slippery and complex. Level descriptors should, therefore, be regarded not rigidly but as developmental (we may be able to improve on what has been developed) and in the nature of guides rather than dictates. However, it is worth noting that the 'bluntness' of level descriptors in their generic form can be improved considerably by 'translating' them into the discourse of a discipline or a programme (see Chapter 4).

Greater transparency reveals discrepancies

We suggested above that the use of level descriptors is an endeavour to make higher education more transparent. When a system becomes more transparent, it is not unusual that inconsistencies are unearthed. When we did not use any measure that allowed us to make comparisons (institution with institution, programme with programme and so on), we could pretend that there were no inconsistencies. Subjectivity is implicit in a system in which, for example, external examiners for a programme are generally chosen by those working on the programme. Blunt as level descriptors may be, it is possible to use them as a tool to demonstrate that the expectations of achievements of learners on one programme are less than, more than or similar to those on another programme.

In addition to demonstrating anomalies in standards, the introduction of a levels structure creates other difficult questions. For example, the Postgraduate Certificate in Education (PGCE)* is postgraduate in terms of when a student studies for it. However, the actual demands of the learning involved – which we might therefore assume to be at Master's level – may not match the Master's level descriptors. One way of dealing with the situation is to distinguish, therefore, between programmes that are postgraduate in time and those that are postgraduate in level, and to recognize that new learning does not require to be pitched at or above the level at which learning has already been achieved. It is reasonable to learn more at the same level or at a lower level. Issues such as this are addressed in the Qualifications Framework, but as we have shown earlier, because of the lack of reference to credit, there remain problems in describing the nature of qualifications in what might be considered sufficient detail to ensure reasonable comparability across the institutions.

Another form of discrepancy revealed by attention to level is the anomaly of modules offered at two different levels. It has been quite usual, for example, for students at level 2 to be offered the same modules with the same learning outcomes, and assessment at level 2 or level 3. In such cases the level of award of the credit has depended on the level of the student and not on the level of difficulty of the module reflected in the learning outcomes (see Chapter 5). Use of a levels system requires modules, their learning outcomes

---

* This is now to become the Professional Certificate in Education.

and assessment criteria to be identified with one level depending on the learning challenge of the learning.

Similarly *ab initio* learning can pose a problem within a system of levels. Within a Master's programme, for example, a student might study a completely new language (for example, classical languages in a theology Master's). The issue is whether a completely new subject can addressed directly at Master's level. As with some of the situations above, there are ways around this. One is to argue that Master's level learners will achieve the learning outcomes more proficiently and rapidly because they can function at Master's level and thus label the studies as Master's level. Another method is to allow for a certain number of credits to be studied at a lower level than the level of a qualification: so at Master's level it may be appropriate for 30 credits to be achieved at lower than Master's level.

There are more subtle anomalies that arise as a result of using an agreed system of levels. For example, we tend to talk about a module or a short course being at a certain level when the learning outcomes in that module generally match that reflected in a set of level descriptors. We might use the same descriptors also to talk about a qualification being awarded at the same level when the programme is completed at that level. Thus a short course (eg of two weeks' duration) might be at level 3, while an honours degree student's achievement is matched against the same level descriptors when she has spent 20 weeks studying at that level. This kind of anomaly is again an argument for viewing level descriptors as 'guides to achievement' rather than specifying that they represent threshold standard for attainment at the end of a level. This parallels the conceptual difficulty that the QAA qualification descriptors confront, when a number of different qualifications are completed within one level (see earlier).

Issues that concern articulation

The decision to adopt any one system of level descriptors with a certain number of levels may pose a set of problems that concern the connection of that system with others where students transfer to or from institutions. One example relates to Scotland and other countries which work on systems of four undergraduate levels. Another concerns the relationship of further education levels to higher education. I have indicated that level descriptors such as NICATS descriptors (from Northern Ireland) include further education levels in the same system, thereby avoiding the problem. The metaphor of a 'seamless system' has been applied in these situations.

Articulation between the different systems of levels that are available is another concern. I have suggested that there are conceptual differences between QAA qualification level descriptors and credit level descriptors. Institutions will feel the need to pay some heed to the qualification level descriptors because they represent the 'language' of any quality review procedures and they are the descriptors that the reviewers will use. However, such descriptors are not necessarily the best option, in terms of format and detail, to use to underpin programme design or to facilitate the writing of learning outcomes, and there may be a wish to use two systems for their different qualities. However, then the equivalence becomes relevant. The choice of a system of level descriptors will be considered in the next section.

Practical issues

Choosing a set of level descriptors

The basis on which a decision is made as to which set of level descriptors to use in an institution will depend to some extent upon local circumstances and the nature of the provision. However, there are some general considerations. The first is, as we have said, that, while QAA indicated that it was content for institutions to choose their own set of level descriptors, QAA reviewers are likely to relate qualifications in an institution to the Qualifications Framework qualification descriptors.

Beyond the function of QAA reviews, however, there are different ways in which level descriptors may be used in higher education, and these require different degrees of detail in the descriptors. For some purposes, such as administration and validation, relatively brief descriptors are adequate and do not generate confusion. The descriptors are required as brief reference points. For other purposes in educational development, such as the writing of learning outcomes, and enabling new lecturers to understand the level of the learning that they should be expecting of learners, more detail is desirable. In addition, with the initiatives in skills development in HE it can be useful to work with level descriptors that make reference to skills and to their development within programmes.

The QF descriptors are relatively brief and do not refer to skills. While they might satisfy administrative purposes, they do not provide the detail that is useful in educational or staff development. On the basis of these points, a compromise would seem to be to adopt the QF descriptors, and to endorse the use of more detailed descriptors for the purposes of staff and educational development. It is important for staff to feel confident in using either set of descriptors, while recognizing their different functions.

In terms of the more detailed descriptors for general areas of higher education provision, the SEEC credit level descriptors adequately fulfil requirements. They are formatted in a helpful manner. They have the same levels structure as the QAA descriptors, and they make reference to skills. Usefully also, the categorization of the descriptors relates to common systems for writing learning outcomes (in terms of knowledge/understanding, cognitive skills and other key or transferable skills). If, however, two sets of level descriptors are used in order to fulfil satisfactorily the different purposes for level descriptors, it is important to consider the comparability of the two sets. Appendix 3 provides a comparison between the SEEC credit level descriptors and QF qualification descriptors. This comparison suggests that there is reasonable compatibility between these descriptors.

Related to the choice of level descriptors is the choice of terminology to be used for level descriptors. The fact that qualification descriptors are conceptually different from credit level descriptors makes the use of one terminology more complex (see below). The set of terms probably most regularly in use in higher education institutions comprises HE 1, 2, 3, Masters and taught doctorate levels, and it is appropriate to begin also to use the qualification levels terminology for whole qualifications.

Different views of descriptors

The next chapter will indicate a range of uses for level descriptors, but it is important to be aware that people can perceive descriptors in different ways. This difference of opinion has become evident from discussion with representatives from various institutions. There is one view in higher education that credit level descriptors make a statement about qualities that *should* be present in higher education programmes, and there is another view that the descriptors indicate what *could* be present. On the basis of the first view, some of the uses of descriptors in the next chapter that suggest the customizing of level descriptors may not be appropriate. This book is written on the basis of a common-sense interpretation of the second view, that the descriptors indicate that where qualities are present, they are provided at the level indicated. In fact, most of the descriptors in SEEC credit level descriptors are present in most higher education provision.

4 Some uses of level descriptors

Introduction

This chapter will indicate a range of uses for level descriptors. All of the different uses contribute ultimately to ensuring that a module, course or a full programme presents learners with an appropriate level of challenge in their learning. This challenge should accord with the levels system in higher education described in earlier chapters. The uses usually apply most directly to the development of modules. Sometimes, however, they also apply to fully developed courses that require to be credit rated at a particular level. The credit rating of a course means that the course is worth a certain volume of academic credit at a given level.

We discussed in the previous chapter the different forms of level descriptors, and in particular the existence of credit level descriptors and the qualification level descriptors that relate to the Qualifications Framework. Since the diversity of uses of level descriptors is largely represented in the realm of educational development, a set of credit level descriptors will be more appropriate for most of the uses discussed below than the qualification level descriptors.

The following are some general guidelines that will support their use.

- Level descriptors should be seen as helpful guides rather than dictates.
- They are generic and may contain sections that are not appropriate to a particular programme. It is reasonable in these circumstances to ignore or remove such sections. For example, psychomotor skills in the older SEEC/HECIW descriptors were not appropriate to all programmes (see previous chapter). It would be unlikely that more than one or two sections would require to be removed.
- There may be areas of learning that are not in the descriptors but that are represented progressively in a particular programme. It

is appropriate to add these to the descriptors, describing them according to expectations of student achievement. One example might be graphic skills, which is an area of function that is central to some programmes such as architecture, but which is not specified in generic descriptors.

- In working with descriptors at a particular level in a programme it is important to look at equivalent descriptors for the previous and the next level. Descriptors work better when viewed in the context of progression – the words become more meaningful.
- In a similar way, in considering a particular descriptor, other descriptors at the same level need to be taken into account. Most of the forms of learning described in level descriptors do not function independently of each other. For example, the ability to analyse at a particular level is meaningless in terms of level unless the complexity of the material of learning is taken into account. A child of five can analyse; what differs from analysis at level 2 is not just the analytical skill, but also the complexity of the material (knowledge and understanding) that the learner is analysing.
- Level descriptors may also be helpful in providing appropriate vocabulary for discussion of areas within the process of learning. This can be useful in any form of description of a programme, in writing learning outcomes, programme outcomes and so on.
- It is important here to reiterate that learning is a 'slippery' subject matter to describe, and words are blunt instruments. We can only do our best in working with level descriptors to describe learning better than it is described in a situation where no such descriptors exist.

The uses of level descriptors are described under the following headings:

- Level descriptors characterize qualifications in higher education.
- They provide a structure for the design of higher education provision.
- They help to maintain standards.
- They can act as indicators of standards in multidisciplinary or non-traditional programmes.

- Level descriptors provide structure for external articulation or accreditation of external awards.
- They provide a means of communication about higher education.
- They are used in curriculum design and development.
- They are a tool for staff development.
- Level descriptors act as a tool for mapping skills and other curriculum components.

Some uses of level descriptors

Level descriptors characterize qualifications in higher education

This use of level descriptors has largely been covered elsewhere, but it is important to recognize it as one of the main uses of level descriptors. In this case, the qualification descriptors will be of particular use.

Level descriptors provide a structure for the design of higher education provision

Levels and level descriptors provide a structure to higher education by giving a more practical meaning to the idea of progression in learning. It is most usual for students to complete a batch of modules at one level before proceeding to modules at the next level, but there can be exceptions to this. We have mentioned situations in which modules predominantly at one level are accompanied by a limited number of modules at a lower level. There are also occasions where students at levels 2 and 3 might tackle a mixture of level 2 and level 3 modules which are delivered in alternate years. This is usually because the number of students is insufficient to enable all modules to be delivered every year. There are occasions, too, on which a learner – usually on a multidisciplinary programme or a student-designed programme and usually part time – may be able to study modules at any level at any stage of a programme. This is allowed so long as credit requirements are fulfilled at the stage of receipt of the qualification. Thus, under guidance, and depending on regulations, an undergraduate may be able to study a topic in modules at levels 1, 2 and 3 over two years, and go back to study another topic in a similar sequence of levels in the next year. Such an arrangement would need to be justified on the basis of appropriate progression and would need to comply with institutional regulations.

The manner in which level descriptors provide structure to higher education is particularly important when students are working towards an award or qualification by accumulating credit from different sources. The description of learning in relation to its level can provide a logical structure for learning when the learning is not overseen by any one provider. Discussion of the accreditation of prior learning (see below) is relevant to this.

Level descriptors help to maintain standards

The maintenance of standards in higher education is subject to many variables. The level of the learning is an important variable here. Relating or developing educational provision to agreed level descriptors means that consistency can be broadly ascertained:

- between similar subject programmes in different institutions;
- between different subject programmes in the same institution;
- where necessary, between providers in different countries;
- between modules and courses.

Particularly significant is the role of level descriptors as a basis for discussion or ascertainment of standards where external reviewers or external examiners are involved.

Level descriptors can act as indicators of standards in multidisciplinary or non-traditional programmes

Multidisciplinary and non-traditional programmes (eg work-based programmes) provide an example of a particular application of level descriptors. Such programmes may not have the usual reference points for quality that are available for more traditional programmes (eg appropriate benchmark statements, professional, vocational, subject body expectations, or even similar other programmes for comparison elsewhere). Demonstration that the learning relates to appropriate levels may therefore be an important mark of quality. Such a quality indicator is more useful if level descriptors are translated into words that relate to the actual programme (see below). We return to these issues in discussion of programme specifications and programme outcomes in Chapter 9.

Level descriptors provide structure for external articulation or accreditation of external awards

There are more often now situations in higher education where an institution needs to relate provision or learning that has been external to it, to its own provision. A situation that affects individuals is the accreditation of prior learning or of prior experiential learning (APL or APEL). In the former situation, typically a learner will present with an award or several awards from previous courses and ask for advanced standing on a programme that she wants to pursue. The receiving institution will consider the nature of the awards, the appropriateness of their level and the content of the learning referenced in learning outcomes in relation to the new programme. Sometimes a decision might be made that the learner will be required to present more work. Level descriptors can be important in deciding the nature of the additional work. Accreditation of prior experiential learning relates to situations that are similar but in which the prior learning is not formally accredited. In this case the learning outcomes and their level need to be ascertained by consideration of level descriptors.

In another situation, providers of relatively advanced short courses developed outside higher education may request that the course is accredited as a higher education award. This will usually mean that it is assessed as being worth so many credits at a particular level. Learners who attain the award might then want to present it in an APL situation and use it towards another (greater) award or qualification. In such situations, level descriptors may be used to communicate with providers the level of difficulty of learning that will be required in order to accredit the course at a particular level, or they may be used to ascertain the level at which the course will be accredited.

Level descriptors provide a means of communication about higher education

Level descriptors provide a means of communication about the expectations of the learning in higher education between, for example:

- staff in the same subject area;
- staff in different disciplines;
- staff in the same discipline in different institutions;
- staff and students;
- staff and students and future employers;
- staff and others outside higher education who might provide or make use of short courses.

We have indicated that in their work on the development of the National Qualifications Framework, the QAA reported that many employers and others outside higher education do not understand qualifications in higher education and what they should expect of students at different levels. One reason behind the development of the descriptors associated with the QF and qualification descriptors is to improve communication. For some audiences, a 'translation' of the educational language can be appropriate.

Level descriptors can be used to improve communication with students, again if the language is made to be suitably accessible. It is helpful for students to understand the educational issues that underpin the development of their programmes. This may apply particularly to mature students who can feel very unsure as to what will be expected of them in higher education when they have not engaged in such processes for many years. Discussion of the expected learning in relationship to level descriptors can bring to notice some issues that can prove to be problematic for students. Level descriptors may enable students to formulate questions about the standards expected in their work. One example of this concerns vocabulary. There is disagreement about meaning among staff over some terms in use in higher education, examples being 'reflective practice', 'critical analysis' and 'independent study'. If staff cannot reach agreed meanings about such a vocabulary, essay titles with such a word may cause confusion even if the confusion is not voiced. The use of level descriptors accompanied by discussion of the word meanings and implications can be very helpful to students – and staff.

Sometimes the beginning of a programme is not the best time at which to discuss such material other than in a very cursory manner. A more suitable time is a short way into the course when students are more attuned to what is happening and they have settled a little. We sometimes introduce too much too early in induction periods, when students may often have overrun their capacity to deal with new ideas.

In the section on staff development, later in this chapter, we suggest some activities that both encourage discussion among staff, and yield materials that are valuable in communication about levels and expectations of learning.

Level descriptors are used in curriculum design and development

Level descriptors have an important role to play in the development of modules or courses, as we suggested in the previous chapter. Figure 2.1 provides a map of course or module development showing the role of level descriptors. While, in practice, it is unlikely that courses or modules will be developed by looking first at the level descriptors alone, often a module will be developed from a general aim and a notion of the level at which the module is to be presented.

The model suggests that the level descriptors are translated into subject descriptors by translating the generic descriptors into subject-specific language. While this procedure is not essential, it has much value in providing a more precise description of level that is directly relevant to the curriculum under development. The development becomes a more meaningful representation of what this group of students is expected to achieve, in terms that this group of staff can feel that they own and completely understand. The discussion about vocabulary (above) is relevant here. Some further tips about using such an exercise are listed below.

Whether or not level descriptors are translated into subject descriptors, we demonstrate in the next chapter how they are used alongside aims to guide the writing of learning outcomes. Aims are teaching intentions about the material that will be covered or how it will be covered. They might also detail the management of the input into a module or course. Thus a combination of level descriptors and aim cover content and the standard of the coverage. Learning outcomes concern the output of learning: what a learner is expected to know, understand or be able to do at the end of a module/course. A definition of a learning outcome might reasonably suggest that it should be written in conjunction with level descriptors (see Chapter 5). In turn, as we have indicated, learning outcomes also imply assessment criteria. In reviewing the links between levels, learning outcomes and assessment criteria, any aspect of the system can be modified in order to improve articulation – except the agreed level descriptors.

Level descriptors are a tool for staff development

This first paragraphs of this section suggest some general staff development activities on levels and level descriptors, while the second part discusses one of these activities in greater detail.

One of the difficulties of introducing level descriptors to staff is to help them to 'get inside' the descriptors. Until there is a good reason for working with descriptors, there is a tendency to 'look at them' as opposed to getting a feel for what they are really saying. In a vicious circle, not having 'a feel for them' is a reason why they might not be used at a later stage when their use would be appropriate. Below is a set of exercises that encourage staff in a staff development session to focus on the meaning of the descriptors and also, this time as a by-product, to produce documents that have a value *per se*.

- Compare SEEC credit level descriptors with QF qualification level descriptors. What differences are there? What are the implications of the differences, given the different purposes for which the descriptors were developed?
- Pick the descriptors for one level in a set of descriptors, and use them as the basis of an information sheet for students about the standards of learning that are expected of them at that level. Broadly maintain the headings used in the descriptors. The outcome of this exercise is particularly helpful for Master's level students who may be returning to a formal learning situation after many years and often do not feel that they know what is expected of them.
- Go through a set of credit level descriptors and extract words that

you feel require some further explanation. Compile a glossary which includes agreed definitions of these more difficult words. Bear in mind as you write the definitions that they must also apply to the word where it appears at other levels in the descriptors.

■ Translate a set of descriptors into the discourse of your discipline, subject or programme. We describe this exercise in greater detail below.

When staff work with level descriptors, they may engage in conversations about their expectations of the learners in their modules or on their programme that would not normally occur. Such conversations are particularly useful during the development of the modules for a new programme, or in situations where staff do not spend time with each other talking in general terms about the learners and their learning processes. One of the best ways to encourage such engagement is to ask a group of staff on a programme, or from a similar subject area, to translate levels represented in their programme into the discourse of their programme. The SEEC credit level descriptors are particularly suitable for this exercise because of the systematic detail and labelling systems under which the descriptors are structured. Working in this way means that staff have to discuss, for example, what they mean by educational words such as 'analysis' in their modules or programme; or they will discuss if or how particular skills (eg presentation skills) feature and whether or not they should be present.

The translation exercise is best when all levels in a programme are tackled, but the level of the qualification should be the first considered so that it sets statements of the level of work ultimately to be attained. If the SEEC descriptors are used, with a large group of staff, the different areas of level descriptors can be tackled by sub-groups, probably of no more than six staff members. The translated materials can then be circulated in a consultation exercise aimed at improving the precision of the words and ensuring that there is coherence across the descriptors for each level. Where several levels are tackled, the wording of the same area of each level needs to be consistent in order for it to be meaningful in terms of progression of learning. It has been observed in practice that the translation of the areas of knowledge and understanding represents a more difficult task than the translation of skills, and where a small group is working on all of the descriptors, skill areas are better tackled first.

It is important to indicate to staff undertaking this exercise that it is possible that not all of the descriptors will be relevant to their programme, and that it is all right to discard areas of description if they are not represented. Equally it is possible that capacities or skills that are not represented in the generic descriptors are important in the programme and thus should be added.

In doing this exercise, staff will not only be learning about level and learning how colleagues think about level and vocabulary, but they will also be developing an important document for future reference in monitoring or review situations – or as a basis for the development of other modules.

Level descriptors act as a tool for mapping skills and other curriculum components

Sets of level descriptors, such as the SEEC credit level descriptors, make reference to many skills and other desirable components in higher education programmes. We have indicated that it is not necessary to consider that a programme should represent every area of level descriptors. However, the generic layout of the range of expected student learning that is common in most programmes can provide the basis for mapping the content of these within a programme at each level.

Concluding comment

This chapter has indicated that there are many ways in which level descriptors can be used to construct appropriate provision in higher education. With the new introduction of the Qualifications Framework, it seems likely that there could initially be some difficulties in deciding which set of descriptors to adopt or how to combine the use of two sets (qualification descriptors and credit level descriptors). As much as anything else, it is likely to be the degree of detail that is required that will determine which kinds of descriptors are used.

The next chapter concerns learning outcomes which should be written with level in mind.

5 Writing and using aims and learning outcomes

Introduction

An example of a learning outcome is:

Example 1

At the end of reading this chapter the reader is expected to be able to produce effective learning outcomes for a module in higher education, pointing out the main components of the learning outcomes.

The map of module development is repeated in order to demonstrate the context of aims and learning outcomes within the process of module development.

The role of the aim in module development is to provide direction and orientation in terms of content for the writing of learning outcomes, while the standard and degree of learning challenge in a learning outcome is drawn from the level descriptors. Most of this chapter will concern learning outcomes since they are more central to the processes under discussion, as we now focus on learning rather than teaching (D'Andrea, 1999). Aims tend to be associated with objectives, and the chapter will briefly consider objectives and provide some reasons for abandoning their use.

The ideas behind learning outcomes

The history of ideas

The outcomes-based approach to learning and programme and module development had its origins in the work of the behavioural psychologists in the early part of the twentieth century. Their influence has eventually shifted the orientation of teachers from

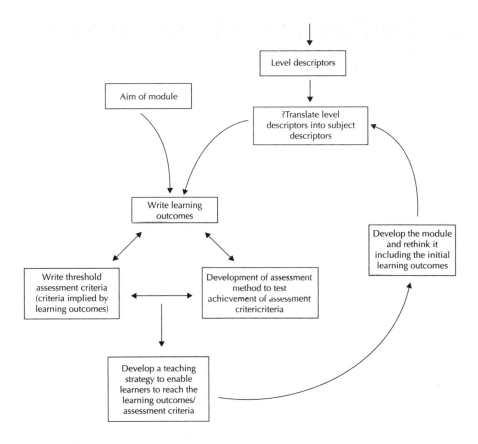

Figure 5.1   Basic map of module development

teaching to learning, though the association of this shift with the unpopular behaviourist movement might not be generally welcomed!

In the middle part of the last century a number of behaviourists became interested in the teaching / learning situations in school, and developed ideas of programmed learning that was delivered through teaching machines. The 'delivery' of teaching in this manner necessitated the deconstruction of material into sequences of appropriately linked ideas. From this developed the 'learning technology' movement, with Mager as one of its best known proponents (Mager, 1975). Mager wrote about the writing of what he called 'instructional objectives'. These objectives were more or less what we would now call 'learning outcomes'. The ideas were then applied in pockets of provision (eg Stones and Anderson, 1972) and became particularly associated with 'objective' assessment and programmed learning. The rapid development of computer technology began to take forward the ideas of programmed learning in more sophisticated ways, still with learning at the centre. Interestingly now there are signs that some areas of technology have become increasingly focused back on teaching, presentation and instruction as the current passion for elaborate and 'good-looking' web sites has emerged.

A second line of development of outcomes-based approaches came about from the developing concern with skills shortages and the perceived poverty of vocational education. Following analyses of occupational activities and competences, systems of national vocational qualifications (NVQs) were developed. NVQs describe how a person is required to demonstrate competence in a particular area, and there is no indication about what instruction needs to be used to enable the reaching of that level of competence.

The third development of outcomes-based learning came about as a result of the credit development movements in the UK in the early part of the 1990s. Credit was not always outcomes-based, but in the projects to which reference has been made in Chapter 1, the volume of learning is based on the notional time taken to achieve given learning outcomes at a specified level (Moon, 1995c). As we have described earlier, it is primarily this source of influence that has led to the widespread use of learning outcomes in higher education at present. However, in considering learning outcomes now, it is useful to recognize the existence of the related developments. They have often been the source of negative reactions to the use of learning outcomes. As I have described, in the first workshops on learning outcomes, the assumed link between learning outcomes and NVQs generated much antipathy, and still the charge is being made that learning outcomes are mechanistic and destroy the real essence of learning (Allan, 1996). In a way these are helpful arguments. It is important that higher education continues to recognize that the good qualities of good learning are those that cannot necessarily be specified in advance (Otter, 1992; Broadfoot, 2000). It is important in the use of learning outcomes that we tread an appropriate path between precision in specification of learning and the openness to unexpected areas of learning. A significant principle here is that learning outcomes should be written at threshold. This matter will be discussed at length in later parts of this chapter.

The role of learning outcomes

The use of learning outcomes and associated threshold assessment criteria provides a mechanism for describing learning either in prospective terms – to be achieved – or in retrospective terms – learning that has been achieved already. The main example here is of learning outcomes, usually within modules, that are accumulated for a qualification. In individual terms, an example of retrospective uses of learning outcomes is in the accreditation of prior experiential learning (APEL).

Learning outcomes should be closely related to assessment criteria. The two sets of statements should work together so that it is often the case that a more general kind of learning outcome statement is supported with more detailed assessment criteria. Where the outcome statement is written in a relatively precise and focused manner, the role of assessment criteria may be less critical.

While the principal purpose of learning outcomes concerns standards of student learning, and the relationship of learning to assessment, there are many other ways in which such statements may be used once they have been written. It is worth bearing in mind the purposes for learning outcomes when they are being written, because these may affect such factors as the use of words. For example, the audience for the learning outcomes may need to be considered if communication of the learning outcomes to a lay audience (eg employers) is a primary concern. This might imply the explanation of more technical words or an accompanying glossary.

Some of the broader purposes for which learning outcomes might be used are:

- They make it possible to be explicit about what is expected of the learner in terms of learning to be attained and the assessment.
- They provide a means of indicating to learners the link between their learning and the manner in which learning is to be assessed.
- They can provide an indication of the standards that the individual teacher or the higher education community expects of

learners, particularly if the relationship of the learning outcomes to level descriptors is made explicit.

- They are a good way of communicating the learning purpose that the module is intended to fulfil. They provide information to other teachers, students and employers (etc) and they can be used within marketing material.
- They can be a useful tool for communication with external examiners.
- The use of learning outcomes provides a means of judging and attaining consistency of volumes and standards of learning within and across institutions, particularly with regard to the same subject material.
- Learning outcomes at level 3 might be compared with the subject benchmark statements for the subject, in order to determine how closely the latter are being followed (see later). Subject benchmarks do not have to be followed by subject teachers, but the rationale for an alternative approach should be justified (QAA, 2000c).
- In the context of a credit-based higher education system, learning outcomes are part of the definition of credit, as part of the measure of volume of learning.
- In providing information about what a learner has achieved, a set of learning outcomes is a kind of transcript.
- Skills and other components of learning can be identified within a module from an observation of the language in which learning outcomes are described. A map of skills within a programme can then be developed.
- Sometimes it is useful to use special standard learning outcomes across all modules in a level so that, for example, specific skills or issues of plagiarism are addressed in an agreed and consistent manner (see examples below).

Some related developments: subject benchmarks and programme specifications

While we return to subject benchmarks and programme specification in Chapter 9, they do have some relationships to learning outcomes and therefore should be mentioned here. Benchmarks may, for example, influence the manner in which learning outcomes are constructed.

Subject benchmarks are, in effect, generalized statements of the learning outcomes that might be achieved by a student completing an honours degree in a particular subject area. The initiative followed the recommendation of the Dearing Committee (NCIHE, 1997), and the work on the benchmarks has been published by the QAA over several years. Forty-two subjects and subject areas were identified for the process of development of the benchmarks. Expert groups, drawn from across the UK, were charged with the task of constructing the statements, initially at threshold level and later to describe the performance of the average or typical student. Some subject benchmark groups also described excellent students. The first three groups worked on law, chemistry and history.

Subject benchmark statements are written (at present) just for the honours degree level, and are likely to be most influential on learning at level 3, and hence for learning outcomes written for modules at level 3. Benchmarks should, of course, influence the writing of learning outcomes only if they are a fair reflection of the content of the learning. Similarly, if benchmark statements do influence the manner of writing learning outcomes for level 3, this form of writing should be demonstrated in the progression from level 1. Even if the benchmark statements are not so helpful for a particular programme because it draws from more than two disciplines, they can be useful as a source of appropriate vocabulary for the subject in question. The subject benchmarks are available from the QAA www site (QAA, www).

Dearing also promoted the idea of a programme specification, which amounts to the design of a common format for the description of all higher education programmes. The format encompasses many similar characteristics to the forms used to describe modules, including material about level, aims, curriculum, teaching, learning and assessment information and sources of maintenance of standards (etc) (QAA, 2000c). Of relevance to this chapter on learning outcomes is the section on 'programme outcomes'.

Generally speaking, the term 'learning outcome' has been applied to the outcomes of relatively small blocks of learning such as those that emanate from modules or short courses. Programme outcomes are outcomes-based statements about the whole programme, and therefore encompass more than simply the sum of the learning outcomes for modules in the highest level of a qualification. When they are written for honours degree programmes, it is also expected that they will pay some regard to the subject benchmark statements. These issues are discussed in a broader context within Chapter 9.

Definition and examples of learning outcomes

In terms of definition, a learning outcome is:

> a statement of what a learner is expected to know, understand and be able to do at the end of a period of learning and of how that learning is to be demonstrated. Learning outcomes are linked to the relevant level and since they should generally be assessable they should be written in terms of how the learning is represented.

Sometimes the definition of a learning outcome is written in terms of 'the learner will (be able to do something)...'. In these days of litigation, it is safer to use the notion of 'expected to be able...' since a teacher has no real control over a student's learning. The student may simply not turn up to lectures. An alternative approach to the word 'expected' is a tentative form of terminology such as 'intended' or 'anticipated' learning outcomes. In any case, the principle is that no one can make a student learn; we can only hope that learning will occur. The existence of a learning outcome that states that a student will learn something does not ensure that the student gets out of bed to come to the lecture. This matter is one of those that emphasize the difference between the activities of teaching and learning – and that learning is something only the student can control.

Learning outcomes do not usually specify curriculum details, but they refer to more general areas of learning. There may be an exception to this in science and applied science subjects (see the next section). However, as a 'rule of thumb' it is unlikely that there will be more than eight learning outcomes per module. If there are more than ten, they are probably specifying too much curricular detail and may then be unmanageable in the process of assessment.

Ironically, the suggested number of eight as a maximum for learning outcomes could apply to a day course or a three-semester module if both are, in effect, the size of unit that will be assessed at one time. In other words, there is no common practice in the size of the 'chunks' of learning that are written as learning outcomes, and the result is that on a shorter course, there may be fewer learning outcomes and they will tend to be more detailed.

I have indicated before that it is important to relate learning outcomes to a level where they are relevant. One implication of this is that it is not appropriate to use the same learning outcomes for a module that may be delivered at two different levels. It is all right for the teaching of a module to be common to students at two levels, and even the actual assessment task can be similar, but the learning outcomes and the assessment criteria will reflect the actual level and will differ between the two modules.

The examples of learning outcomes that follow are numbered. The first example is that found at the beginning of this chapter. They are numbered for purposes of reference in later chapters in this book, in particular Chapter 6 on assessment criteria, in which criteria associated with these learning outcomes are given as examples for that chapter. In some cases, comments are made about specific features in the learning outcomes.

Examples of learning outcomes

Example 2: level 2 BEd programme

At the end of the module the learner is expected to be able to:

explain the more common reasons for difficult behaviour in primary school children in class situations, indicating standard techniques for ameliorating that behaviour

or: within the context of a class situation, demonstrate and evaluate the use of appropriate examples of positive reinforcement for the purpose of the improvement of behaviour.

Example 3: level 3 English literature

At the end of the module, the learner is expected to be able to:

demonstrate detailed understanding of the influences of the historical and social context within which the chosen text is set, both from the study of the text itself and from the study of other contemporary literature.

(Comment: this learning outcome could mention the text by name, but by focusing on the skills to be acquired, one avoids being tied to the same text in the future. In addition, the learning outcome is about learning in more general terms than the specific text.)

Example 4: level 2 physics

At the end of the module, the learner is expected to be able to:

perform correctly calculations on wave functions and in the solution of the Schroedinger equation for a range of one-dimensional problems.

Example 5: level 3 physics

At the end of the module the learner is expected to be able to:

describe and explain the function of the basic devices of optoelectronics; optical fibres; liquid crystal displays; bi-polar and surface field effect transistors and MOS light emitting diodes.

Example 6: level 3 mathematics

At the end of the module, the student will be expected to be sufficiently familiar with the techniques of multivariate analysis in order to be able to handle straightforward multivariate data sets in practice.

Example 7: level 3 independent studies

At the end of the module, the learner will be expected to have developed an agreed set of learning outcomes for a 2,500 word project, based on level descriptors for a level 3 learner, and to demonstrate that she has achieved the outcomes and completed the project to the reasonable satisfaction of her tutor.

(Comment: in this learning outcome, the project learning outcomes will be written by the learner, and hence the learning will relate to the descriptors which will, in a sense, dictate the criteria and the manner in which the module is set up – ie the rationale for an independent studies module.)

Example 8: level 1: a skills module on academic writing for any student

At the end of this module, the student will be expected to be able to explain and demonstrate the main features of effective academic essay at level 1.

Example 9: use of a learning outcome to alert students to potential plagiarism (based on Gosling and Moon, 2001) – could be in any discipline, level 1

At the end of the period of learning, it is intended that the student will be able to discuss how plagiarism can occur intentionally or unintentionally in academic work, and identify ways of avoiding it through appropriate referencing.

Example 10: Master's level, social policy

At the end of the module, learners will be expected to be able to describe the historical development of social policy and judge the value of key developments in health care from the perspective of social policy.

Example 11: Master's level, reproductive health

At the end of the module, learners will be expected to be able to appraise the consequences of a range of key socio-cultural influences on sexual and reproductive health (including sexually transmitted diseases, adolescent sexuality, female genital mutilation, the effects of culture and media).

Example 12: Master's level, learning log module in a leadership programme

At the end of the module, in an oral presentation, making reference to their learning journal entries, learners will be expected to evaluate the role of reflection in their work situations, indicating its values and the role or potential role of negative influences. They will be able to indicate how they can improve their use of learning journals in future use.

Example 13: level 1 skills in physics

At the end of the module, students will be able to demonstrate effective grasp of a range of communication skills that will underpin their further studies in physics. These will include maintenance of a physics note-book, preparation of a CV, the ability to read an academic article and discuss it in a brief presentation.

(Comment: it could be argued that example 13 represents more than one learning outcome. By having all the communication skills in one outcome, the implication is that a student failing one part, fails the whole learning outcome. It can be assumed that there will be other learning outcomes for this module, that also represent a number of small tasks.)

Example 14: level 1 introduction to chemistry module

At the end of the module, it is intended that the student will be able to write a concise, clear and tidy report of a laboratory practical that must be laid out in the prescribed format.

Example 15: level 1 introduction to acting/drama programme

At the end of the module, the student will be expected to be able to work with others in small task-orientated groups, participating and interacting in the group in a productive manner for him/herself and for the group as a whole.

Some forms of module may seem to be problematic for description in advance through statements of learning outcome. An example is negotiated learning, or modules that are described as 'independent studies' (see example above) where, as a part of the module, the learner identifies the subject matter to be studied (and represented in a project, essay etc). In such cases the learning outcomes (quite logically) will relate to the learning of the skills of autonomous learning, project skills and other matters that will usually be the rationale for the design of such a module anyway.

The categorization of learning outcomes

Since the Dearing Report (NICHE, 1997) put an emphasis on skills learning in higher education, it has been common practice to categorize learning outcomes into the apparent characteristics of learning to which they refer. These are usually in accordance with the headings used in the SEEC credit level descriptors, so some learning outcomes might refer to subject-specific knowledge and understanding another group might refer to cognitive or core academic skills, and another might refer to other skills (key/transferable, or other terminology).

Although the development of such categorization systems may apparently be justified on the basis of convenience for analysis of the components of a module (see below), there is a logical problem in this procedure. Let us take for an example a cognitive or core academic skill such as analysis. The existence of categorizations suggests that we should be able to describe the analysis processes undergone by, say, a level 2 student, in a statement that is devoid of reference to content or the nature of the material that is being analysed. The statement should simply consider the nature of the analytical processes. However, in reality, the sophistication of analytical skill is largely determined by the complexity of the material that is being analysed. A child of five can analyse, so long as the material for analysis is sufficiently simple. In other words, to describe the analytical skills of a level 2 student is only possible with reference to the complexity of what is probably categorized as 'knowledge and understanding'. On the basis of this argument, it is illogical to try to write learning outcomes that are categorized as described above. The same reasoning lies behind the suggestion that looking at one item in level descriptors alone, without reference to other descriptors, cannot give a good picture of the level implied.

There are, however, practical values in attempting to introduce some categorization of learning outcomes where it comes to key or transferable skills that are developed in modules. As we have indicated earlier, the practical skill content of programmes is a current major concern in higher education. The indication of where skills are developed within modules through reviewing the learning outcomes provides an easy method of mapping the skill content of modules and ultimately of the whole programme. Although skills are related to other abilities, and to some extent (sometimes) to the complexity of the material, it is more possible to write reasonable skills learning outcomes that make sense alone.

On the basis of the paragraphs above, a reasonable suggestion is that a general set of learning outcomes should be written for the module, with the outcomes related to skills either asterisked or drawn up separately.

Learning outcomes, aims and objectives

Chapter 1 described how, in the early days of learning outcomes workshops, one of the major issues concerned the use of learning outcome language in contrast to the aims and objectives that were in common use at the time. Not only did learning outcomes cause upset to a system that, people argued, had only recently been imposed, but there were difficulties in helping people to see the differences between the language of aims and learning outcomes.

The difference between learning outcomes and aims is that aims are written in terms of teaching intention, and/or indicate what it is that the teacher intends to cover in the block of learning (curriculum coverage). Learning outcomes are descriptions of what the learner is expected to learn in the period of learning defined. Learning outcomes should imply the standard of learning expected. This is another example of the distinction between teaching and learning. Aims are more about teaching and the management of learning, and learning outcomes concern the learner learning.

On the basis of most aim statements, it is entirely possible for a lecturer to go into a lecture theatre at the times of the lecture slots, to teach the course and thereby to fulfil the aim whether or not there are any students present. Student learning does not affect the achievement of the aim unless the aim refers to learning, such as 'aiming to encourage…' or, more optimistically, 'enable' learning.

Because teachers set aims and are usually the agents implied in the aim statement, aims are much more under the control of the teacher. Learning outcomes are not under the control of the teacher but are subject to the whim or will of the learner, and hence are subject to the skills of influence and faith, or hope in the teacher that the learner will learn broadly what has been described.

Where do objectives fit in? Basically, the term 'objectives' tends to complicate the situation, because objectives may be written in the terms of teaching intention or expected learning. In other words, they may look like aim statements or learning outcome statements. It is not unusual to find both forms under one heading of 'course objectives'. This means that some descriptions are of the teaching in the module and some are of the learning. Those that are called 'behavioural' or 'learning' objectives are more likely to be written in learning outcome format, but the confusion may still occur. This general lack of agreement as to the format of objectives is a complication, and justifies the abandonment of the use of the term 'objectives' in the description of modules or programmes.

Since learning outcomes and aims have different functions – one being concerned with teaching and the management of learning, and the other with learning – it is useful to write an aim for a module in addition to learning outcomes. An aim can be a statement of general teaching intention and coverage, as well as indicating the content of the module and its relationship to other learning or the whole programme. It may indicate prerequisite or co-requisite modules. In effect, an aim provides direction for the module. Aims do not need to be long statements, and they should certainly take up less space on any form of module description than the learning outcome statements, since the latter is the focus of the module: the learning element and not the teaching.

Some examples of aim statements are:

The aim is to provide an introduction to the application of statistical theory in general insurance.

(mathematics, level 3)

The aim of the module is to introduce students to the basic areas of digital electronics, as they may be encountered in physics instruments, and to provide the necessary theoretical background to carry out experimental investigations.

(physics, level 1)

Students will need effective communication skills to complete many of their modules, and to succeed in a job after they graduate. This module aims to provide students on all of our programmes with an effective and common grounding in (written and interpersonal skills).

(skills module in physics, level 1)

The aim of the module is to review disciplinary issues in the primary school classroom. We will consider the sources of difficult behaviour, and strategies for discipline and control.

(BEd, level 1)

This module will provide a general introduction to European Union law.

(law, level 2)

In this introductory module, students will be introduced to the modular programme as it is run at Pumphrey University. They will be required to consider, justify and organize the design of the programme of study that they will follow in levels 1 and 2 with weekly tutorial support.

(level 1 module on a modular programme)

This module is the dissertation module in Sociology. With appropriate supervision, during this period students will write dissertations on the topics that they have detailed and had approved in their plans.

(a dissertation module in any programme, level 3)

> The aim of this module is to consider basic educational theory and the manner in which it informs health education practices.
>
> (Master's level, MSc in health education/promotion)
>
> This is an independent studies module. The aim is that students should be enabled to gain initial skills of independent study through their work on planning, researching and executing satisfactorily a project that has been approved by their tutors.
>
> (level 2 module, any programme)
>
> This is an introductory module on mathematics for biology students. It is primarily aimed at those students who have not studied mathematics in sufficient depth to cope with requirements in this programme. The continuous assessment will mean that students become exempted from classes once they have reached the required standard.
>
> (level 1 module, biology)
>
> This module follows on from module NNNN (module code), study of which is a prerequisite for entry to this module. This module will aim to cover more advanced and detailed material on the history of landscape, focusing on the study of woodland.
>
> (level 2 in a group of modules on the theme of heritage in the provision of an adult and continuing education scheme)

Writing learning outcomes

The components and language of learning outcomes

A well-written learning outcome is likely to contain the following three components:

- A verb that indicates what the learner is expected to be able to do at the end of the period of learning.
- A word or words that indicate on what or with what the learner is acting. If the outcome is about skills then the word(s) may describe the way the skill is performed (eg 'jump up and down competently').
- A word or words that indicate the nature (in context or in terms of standard) of the performance required as evidence that the learning was achieved.

We use examples 3 and 6 from pages 57 and 58 to exemplify the components of learning outcomes.

In the first example, learners were expected to 'demonstrate detailed understanding of the influences of the historical and social context within which the chosen text is set, both from the study of the text itself and from the study of other contemporary literature'.

The verb is *'be able to demonstrate'* (what the learner has to do).

The words that indicate on what or with what the learner is acting are *'the influences of the historical and social context'* etc.

The words that describe the nature of the performance are *'demonstrate detailed understanding'* and *'the study of the text'* and *'the study of other contemporary literature'*.

Example 6 says, 'At the end of the module, the student will be expected to be sufficiently familiar with the techniques of multivariate analysis in order to be able to handle straightforward multivariate data sets in practice'.

In this example, the verb is complex. It is *'will be sufficiently familiar with'*.

The words that indicate on what or with what the learner is acting are *'the techniques of multivariate analysis'*.

The words *'handle straightforward multivariate data sets'* describe the nature and context of the performance that shows that the learning has been achieved.

The third component of the learning outcome is apt to be omitted. Since it is the component that provides the main links to assessment criteria and level descriptors, its presence is important to ensure the links in the cycle (see Figure 5.1). On occasions when there are very clear assessment criteria that are obviously linked to the learning outcome in other components, the third component may be less important. There will be more discussion of the relevance of this to assessment criteria in the next chapter.

Learning outcomes that are written for different disciplines may differ in their components because of the structures of knowledge. In some areas of science disciplines, there is a generally agreed hierarchy of knowledge, so that the aspect of optoelectronics mentioned in example 5 is likely to be generally acknowledged as level 3 material for physics students. The nature of the subject matter, in such cases, will itself largely determine the level at which the module is offered, and extra words that indicate the depth of knowledge may not be necessary. In contrast, in many humanities and arts subjects, a knowledge component may be encountered in modules at any level, and issues such as the depth or context of the knowledge will indicate the level of the module. An example of this is shown in learning outcome example 12. The text in this learning outcome may be the subject of study at more or less any level. In this case it will be the level of learning challenge, in relation to the sophistication of the learner's knowledge and skills, that will determine the actual level of the module. Greater detail is needed of the way in which the learner must act in order to demonstrate success in achieving the learning outcome.

Some learning outcome statements may not order the components in the same sequence as above, and a learning outcome statement does not need to be written in one sentence alone. However, many learning outcome statements that run into multiple sentences are actually several learning outcomes, and problems may then arise when it comes to the development of appropriate assessment criteria and the designing of assessment tasks. Theoretically there can be a problem when one component of a multiple learning outcome is not achieved satisfactorily, in that the student technically then fails the whole learning outcome.

Another common fault in the writing of learning outcomes is that they refer to learning and not the representation of learning. A poorly written learning outcome might say, for example:

> At the end of the module, the learner will be expected to know the health and safety practices of laboratory work.
>
> (level 1 chemistry)

We can only tell if the student knows these practices if she is caused to demonstrate her knowledge. She might be asked to write a report, to answer questions, to explain the practices orally and so on. A more appropriate form of this learning outcome might be:

Example 16: level 1 chemistry

At the end of the module, the learner will be expected to be able to show to a demonstrator that she has a working understanding of health and safety practices with reference to a specific laboratory experiment, through an oral or written report on this aspect of the experiment.

We assess the representation of learning, not the learning itself. A learner may 'take in' ideas and may have learnt them, but until we can see the ideas represented, we cannot know that the learning has occurred. There will always be different ways in which the same learning can be represented, and learners may be more able at one form of representation than another. A dyslexic student may have learned something but she may be unable to represent it in writing. Learning outcomes need, therefore, to be written in terms of the representation of learning (eg not 'be able to understand', but 'be able to demonstrate understanding of...').

The box on pages 67 to 69 provides some useful vocabulary for writing learning outcomes (and assessment criteria). Some of the words are about the process of learning, and some about the representation of learning. It is often suggested that words like 'understanding' or 'know' should not be used in learning outcomes. The problem is as described above: that only words that refer to the representation of learning will indicate that the learning has been achieved. There is no problem in the use of such words, so long as a means of knowing that the learning has been achieved is present as well. Sometimes it is also appropriate to include other words that modify the learning word (eg 'know thoroughly' or 'know in detail'). The difference between 'know' and 'know thoroughly' will need to be made evident in the assessment criteria.

Some vocabulary for writing learning outcomes and assessment criteria

Finding the right words to use to describe learning can be difficult, particularly when the statements should relate to generic level descriptors. The following list is provided as an aid in this process. The words are organized for convenience under headings that might be seen to accord with those from Bloom's taxonomy. However, no hierarchy is intended. Some words would fit several headings, and individually words cannot be related to a particular level or standard. It should be remembered that a child of eight can synthesize a word from a series of letters: the level of difficulty of the word (ie the complexity of the subject matter), in this case, will determine the level of the task. The list of words below is simply a vocabulary list (gleaned from a variety of sources).

Activities giving evidence of knowing

Define, describe, identify, label, list, name, outline, reproduce, recall, select, state, present, be aware of, extract, organize, recount, write, recognize, measure, underline, repeat, relate, know, match.

Activities giving evidence of comprehension

Interpret, translate, estimate, justify, comprehend, convert, clarify, defend, distinguish, explain, extend, generalize, exemplify, give examples of, infer, paraphrase, predict, rewrite, summarize, discuss, perform, report, present, restate, identify, illustrate, indicate, find, select, understand, represent, name, formulate, judge, contrast, translate, classify, express, compare.

Activities giving evidence of knowledge/understanding

Apply, solve, construct, demonstrate, change, compute, discover, manipulate, modify, operate, predict, prepare, produce, relate, show, use, give examples, exemplify, draw (up), select, explain how, find, choose, assess, practise, operate, illustrate, verify.

Activities giving evidence of analysis

Recognize, distinguish between, evaluate, analyse, break down, differentiate, identify, illustrate how, infer, outline, point out, relate, select, separate, divide, subdivide, compare, contrast, justify, resolve, devote, examine, conclude, criticize, question, diagnose, identify, categorize, point out, elucidate.

Activities giving evidence of synthesis

Propose, present, structure, integrate, formulate, teach, develop, combine, compile, compose, create, devise, design, explain, generate, modify, organize, plan, rearrange, reconstruct, relate, reorganize, revise, write, summarize, tell, account for, restate, report, alter, argue, order, select, manage, generalize, précis, derive, conclude, build up, engender, synthesize, put together, suggest, enlarge.

Activities giving evidence of evaluation

Judge, appraise, assess, conclude, compare, contrast, describe how, criticize, discriminate, justify, defend, evaluate, rate, determine, choose, value, question.

The box on pages 69 to 71 outlines a useful exercise that can act as a summary to a session on the components and language of learning outcomes: or it can act as a self-test for this chapter. The text provides the explanation.

An exercise in distinguishing learning outcomes from teaching intentions (aims)

Introduction

The exercise below is based on documents for the accreditation of a short professional development course in health education submitted to a university. The regulations regarding the submission required a course description in terms of aims and learning outcomes. You will see that there was confusion. *Which are aims, which are learning outcomes?* To complicate matters, many of the learning outcomes are written poorly. As a reminder, there are three components to a well-written learning outcome:

- verb (what the learner will be expected to do);
- what the learner is acting on/with (usually the object of the verb);
- an indication of how one will know that the learner has reached that standard (usually indicated in terms of standard, or in statements about the context or difficulty of the work).

Learning outcomes should also be testable. Think about whether the statements below are what they say they are – aims or learning outcomes – and, if they are anything like the latter, are all of the components present?

Aim 1

The aim is to help participants to develop their role as health educators in their everyday work so that health education is not separated from normal activities.

Learning outcomes

- Participants will be able to describe a range of health education methods that they might use in their work.
- They will be offered the opportunity to explore their existing health education role and identify ways in which they might develop and extend that role.
- They will develop an understanding of the principles and aims of adult learning.
- The programme will enable them to gain basic awareness of methods of planning of health education interventions.

Aim 2

To provide participants with an opportunity to expand their understanding of theoretical and practical aspects of working with groups.

Learning outcomes

- Participants will be able to describe the roles that people tend to adopt when functioning in groups and to discuss the roles in relation to a series of given case students of group functioning.
- Participants will consider the impact of their membership in a variety of personal and professional groups.
- Participants will experience three leadership styles.

- Through role play, they will demonstrate that they are able to cope effectively with the behaviour of difficult group members.

Aim 3

The participants will be able to explain the basic theory of communication skills.

Learning outcomes

- They will be able to show that they can incorporate a range of new communication skills and strategies into their existing competencies.
- They will have explored their current abilities in communication in a variety of settings.

Aim 4

The aim is to equip participants with the skills to use effectively a variety of resources in health education strategies.

Learning outcomes

- To enable participants to learn effective means of using a variety of educational resources.
- The participants will be able to evaluate health education videos for their content and potential audience using the evaluation framework provided on the course.
- Participants will be able to discuss the merits and disadvantages of three (given) health education packs, at least one of which deals with stopping smoking.

Learning outcomes and their location at minimum/threshold standard

Learning outcomes are statements that indicate what is the essential learning, and as essential learning, they are written at minimum acceptable or threshold standard. The learning described in learning outcomes is the learning that must be attained in order that the learner can pass or achieve the learning. Although we do not directly associate the use of learning outcomes and the grading system (see later in this section), in effect, learning outcomes are written at whatever is the mark that distinguishes between pass and fail (and sometimes this mark will be different between under-graduate and postgraduate programmes). It is this point that really stresses the role of learning outcomes in quality assurance.

There are important implications of the paragraph above. The fact that learning outcomes are essential means:

- that a learner attains or fails to attain a learning outcome, and therefore attains or fails to attain 'essential' learning;
- and on this basis if the learner attains some learning outcomes and fails to attain others and then, technically, she fails the module.

In practice many institutions do not operate this system and compensation is allowed. The view is taken that if some outcomes are passed 'well', they can compensate for others that are not passed. Technically this represents a confusion between a grading system and the use of learning outcomes, because learners pass or do not pass essential learning outcomes.

We use the word 'technically' with some consideration here, because it is in this sort of 'regulation-speak' that we are apt to forget how 'woolly' most learning outcomes actually are. Is it possible to tell absolutely without doubt whether a student has attained or not attained a learning outcome? Consider this example:

Example 17: level 1, biology

At the end of the module, the learner will be expected to be able to explain in detail the main functions of the cell wall in algae.

We have said before that we are trying to improve our precision in the matter of managing learning, but we must acknowledge the limitations of this approach. It is a form of word play. The passing or failing of the above learning outcome could be a matter of opinion. The addition of written assessment criteria that indicate the parts of the cell wall that should be mentioned might help if that level of detail was appropriate, but how do you judge the effectiveness of an 'explanation in detail'?

There are, of course, some learning outcomes that provide absolute information about whether they have been passed or failed: for example, those involving calculations that are correct or not correct. We do need a clear system that indicates that learning outcomes are written at threshold, but at the same time we need to recognize the limitations of their precision in practice.

While we have talked above about learning outcomes that are 'essential', it is perfectly possible to write 'desirable learning outcomes'. However they should clearly be labelled as such, and the system well explained to students. Terminology such as 'module learning outcomes' could be helpful in distinguishing desirable from essential learning outcomes. Later in this chapter we suggest a system in which the latter are written formally for identified purposes.

A further implication of the idea that learning outcomes are essential is that any system of grading is a separate operation from passing or failing to pass a learning outcome. Grading is a very common process, but it is usually an option rather than a necessity in most situations in higher education. It might be a necessity if there is a requirement to distinguish between students by their level of achievement within modules (eg where only very competent students are allowed to proceed along a particular path of learning). Grading seems to be used mostly because it provides feedback to students and staff, and because students like to know how they are getting on, rather than only that they have passed or failed (see Chapters 6 and 7). When grading is used, the criterion for attaining a learning outcome will match the pass/fail point for the grading. As we will indicate later, this is the grading assessment criterion on the pass–fail line, with further grading assessment criteria grading above or below this line.

Many people are surprised when they realize that learning outcomes are written at threshold standard. As Chapter 1 showed, it has been a contentious issue in workshops. However the use of such a standard is fully justified in terms of creating a clear relationship between assessment and level of learning. It is, in effect, this relationship in which the notion of the 'standard' of a programme is most strongly represented. The reasoning for this goes back to the difficulty in writing generic level descriptors at threshold standard. If we cannot prescribe the threshold of acceptable attainment in the level descriptors, the 'drawing of this line' has to belong in the standards that are articulated in learning outcomes in modules. Subject benchmark statements have to some (variable) extent taken this role of articulating standards, but they are only available at level 3 and they only 'work' for programmes that adhere closely to the subject matter that they describe.

There is also another important area of reasoning that supports the maintenance of threshold standard for learning outcomes. The reasoning is demonstrated in Figure 5.2.

The figure represents a notional view of student achievement, from 0 to 100 per cent. Writing a learning outcomes threshold standard (or on the pass/fail line – say at 40 per cent) can be said to 'tie down' what is described as the lowest 40 per cent of achievement. It means that that area of learning is prescribed by the learning outcomes, and the learning that is described must be achieved. Learning outcomes at threshold tell the student what she must do in order to pass the module. Writing learning outcomes at threshold in this way forms a sort of contract between the teacher and the student: 'If you achieve these, I will let you pass the module.' It seems completely fair to indicate to a student the standard that she must reach in order to pass. Ironically while many would agree with this latter statement, they then go on to argue that learning outcomes should be written for the 'average' student – and

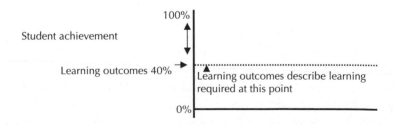

Figure 5.2 Learning outcomes and the qualities of higher education learning

a logical flaw in their argument thereby appears. A theoretical problem arises here as well, in the identification of what 'average' means: is it at 55 per cent or 60 per cent or 65 per cent, or where? In order to relate 'average' to a pass/fail point of 40 per cent, we would need to express it also at a percentage.

An important point is made by this model (Figure 5.2) in terms of the perceived nature of higher education as the opportunity for the exploration of ideas, the development of creative approaches to subject matter and the chance to reflect in an independent manner. In the model, the learning above the threshold or pass/fail line does not have to be 'tied down' in description. In other words, if the pass mark is 40 per cent, we are talking of 60 per cent of the learning being unaffected by the writing of essential learning outcomes, although they will have given an orientation to the learning. It is 'space' in which the higher qualities of higher education learning can be expressed in the student's learning and perhaps within the approaches to teaching and/or the teaching process. Seen in this way, the writing of learning outcomes at threshold is fair to students, provides accountability and a form of liberation of learning, in that it allows for the expression of these higher qualities of higher education learning.

The story does not quite end here because in practice, we tend further to tie down expected learning by the imposition of the system of grading and associated grading assessment criteria. Grading represents a form of system of 'desirable learning outcomes', but for clarity it is probably better not to use the same term, particularly since we will be suggesting its use for a slightly different purpose later in this section.

Learning outcomes and assessment: some further points

While learning outcomes are meant to have a clear relationship to assessment, in practice this tends to be a somewhat confused area. Certainly, all learning outcomes should be assessable; in other words they should be written in terms that enable testing of whether or not the student has achieved the outcome. Furthermore, we have mentioned above that learning outcomes need to be written in the language of representation of learning.

While we can say that all learning outcomes need to be assessable – capable of being assessed – they may not all need actually to be assessed in practice. Whether or not they are all assessed can be an institutional issue, and clearly there are situations in which all learning outcomes do need to be assessed, such as where licence to practice or competence to perform an essential vocational task is concerned.

In other situations, we might accept that we sample learning outcomes. In practice this often happens in examination situations. In an examination paper in which students have a choice as to which questions to answer, they are often not tested on every learning outcome. Since sampling actually happens, it may be more a matter of whether sampling is recognized officially or not. It is probably important to say that all students should at least *expect* to be tested on each learning outcome and should prepare for such testing, even if the chosen assessment method actually samples. However, even the preparation may not occur where learning outcomes are assessed by a choice of coursework essays, and where specific essays may test one or other of the outcome statements.

We have suggested that it may be appropriate to assess a sample of learning outcomes in order to make assumptions about the achievement of all learning outcomes. Theoretically we should be able to assume that all outcomes have been achieved in order to 'pass' the student on a particular module. However, systems of condonement and compensation are common and in practice, as we have suggested, it is usual for examination boards to make allowance for (and, in effect, confuse) by how great a margin a student has passed some learning outcomes, in order to compensate for some clearly not achieved. In such a situation, it is often the case that norm-referenced assessment is creeping into what is technically a criterion-based system (see Chapter 6).

Learning outcomes in vocational programmes

In higher education, most learning outcomes are written for testing directly at the end of a module. Occasionally there is a gap, and a first semester module is assessed at the end of the second semester. However, in the case of much vocational education, the ability of the learner to demonstrate learning at the end of a block of learning (a module or a short course) is of little use. The value of the learning from the module or course is for its application in practice situations in the workplace at a later time. Usually this is long after it is possible for the course organizer to gain access to the learner for assessment purposes, although arrangements with workplace tutors may be made. In effect, the important learning outcomes are really those that might be tested at this later time, but they are often not under the control of the teacher, or designer of the initial programme.

It is usual to expect all learning outcomes to be subject to assessment. However, there may be value in making an exception in this case and writing two sets of learning outcomes. The first set (type 1) can be assessed at the end of the period of learning (module or course). The second set (type 2) can then concern the application of the learning to practical situations in the workplace. They may not actually be tested, but they will provide a 'sense of direction' to the programme, and indicate to learners, those involved in teaching on the module/course, employers and others, the expected standard of practical performance that can be expected to result from the learning.

Another application of thinking of this sort can be applied in a conventional degree situation. Here the learning outcomes from modules may be viewed as type 1 learning outcomes which are then modified by the broadening of knowledge from other modules to become type 2 learning outcomes at the end of a programme. These would not actually be assessed but may be represented by the programme outcomes in a programme specification (see Chapter 9).

Using desirable or aspirational learning outcomes

We have suggested that there are many uses for learning outcomes, and one of these is for marketing an individual module or the modules within a programme or a course. It is evident from discussion from workshops and courses on writing learning outcomes that there is a problem here which creates negativity towards the use of learning outcomes. One kind of comment that is frequently made is that allowing students only to see the minimum expectations can lead to them choosing to work only for the lowest standard to 'get through'. While this is probably true of some students in all institutions, they may often not be the kind of students who will look at learning outcomes anyway. However, a more significant comment is often made that allowing employers to see threshold learning outcomes gives them a poor impression of modules or whole programmes. Clearly one way around this is to separate official module descriptions from publicity material, not using threshold learning outcomes on the publicity material. Another method would be to write some 'aspirational' or 'desirable' learning outcomes for the module or course, that indicate in reasonably formal language what a good student is expected to achieve.

A second, and completely separate, reason for developing 'desirable' learning outcomes is to support the writing of grade assessment criteria, because as the next chapter will indicate, this form of assessment criteria only tenuously relates to learning outcomes at pass/fail point. Hence the learning outcomes written at threshold do not inform very well the writing of such criteria.

6 Writing and using assessment criteria

Introduction

So far in the structuring of programmes, we have considered the roles of levels, level descriptors and learning outcomes. We now come to consider assessment criteria and how they relate both to learning outcomes and assessment methods. By assessment methods, we mean the task undertaken by the student – such as writing an essay, answering a question in an examination or developing a portfolio – that is subject to assessment. Assessment criteria are the basis on which a judgement of the adequacy of the work is made.

In order to illustrate assessment criteria, I shall take the example of a learning outcome presented at the beginning of the last chapter, and develop an assessment method and some assessment criteria. In this chapter references to examples relate to the numbering system developed in Chapter 5.

> Learning outcome (example 1): At the end of reading this chapter the reader is expected to be able to produce effective learning outcomes for a module in higher education, pointing out the main components of the learning outcomes.

In this case, the assessment method is identified and the assessment criteria are written in relation to it. The task could be: to write three learning outcomes that are in a familiar discipline, labelling each with its appropriate level.

Some assessment criteria for the learning outcome above might be:

- The learning outcomes will be written clearly in language that is comprehensible to students at that level in higher education.
- There will be identification of the appropriate level for the learning outcome.
- The reader will be able to point out in the learning outcomes, the three components of learning outcomes discussed in the chapter.

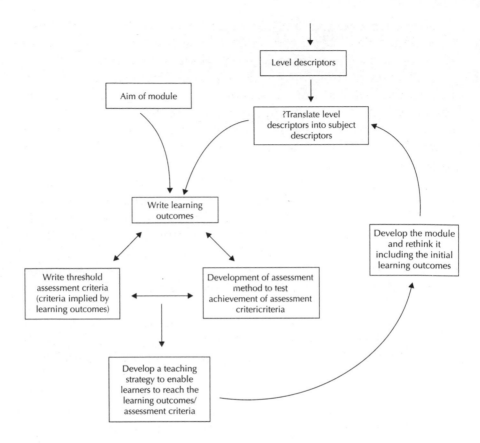

Figure 6.1   Basic map of module development

There are many ways in which to present assessment criteria, and the example above is only one, but it demonstrates how assessment criteria describe the achievement required to demonstrate success in the learning, in greater detail. In writing assessment criteria, it is not always necessary to devise the assessment method prior to the development of assessment criteria, as will be explained. The criteria may be developed with the learning outcomes, leaving the opportunity for different assessment tasks to have been devised. In this example, the readers might have been asked to produce learning outcomes orally or to write one learning outcome and to identify the components in a set of prepared statements. There are many examples in the text of this chapter, in particular in the penultimate section.

As in other chapters in this section of the book, we present the basic map of module development in order to locate the development of assessment criteria in the process of module development (Figure 6.1). As we have indicated above, learning outcomes imply assessment criteria, but in practice assessment criteria may be developed from the learning outcome, or from the task itself. Towards the end of this chapter, we reproduce a version of this model in which grading of assessment is taken into account in the use of grade assessment criteria (Figure 6.2).

The use of assessment criteria implies that a criterion-referenced system for assessment is in place. Criterion-referenced assessment is usually contrasted with norm-referenced assessment, and it is worth at this point clarifying the meaning of the terms. In a criterion-referenced system, the judgement of the learner's work is made on the basis of its quality in relation to predefined criteria: the assessment criteria. A norm-referenced system is based on a prearranged distribution of gradings, or passes and failures, probably in terms of percentages of the whole group. For example, it might be desired to allocate 10 per cent of a group to grade As, 25 per cent to grade Bs, 30 per cent to grade Cs, 25 per cent to grade Ds and 10 per cent to grade Es.

It is not infrequent in higher education that a norm-referenced system quietly underlies and influences what is declared to be a criterion-referenced system. For example, concern about the low or high number of first class honours degrees in several cohorts can encourage adjustment of that number in later cohorts, even in a system that is overtly criterion-referenced. The urge to adjust may be encouraged by the existence of league tables which provide the statistics on 'firsts' to prospective students.

The place of assessment criteria in current higher education

At present the use of effective assessment criteria often seems to be a long way behind the use of learning outcomes and level descriptors. In some institutions the developments could be said to have gone too far, with religious describing of mechanistic criteria following every statement of learning outcome. In other situations, however, in a module description form, the slot that requires some detail about the criteria often elicits information about the assessment method: the details of the length of an examination or the number of words required in an assessed essay. In this situation the criteria, which form the basis for judgement of pass or fail point or marks, tend to reside and continue to reside firmly in the teacher's brain.

There might be review of criteria if, for example, there is some substantial disagreement between a first and second marker. At this point there might be the easy compromise of averaging marks and avoiding the consideration of the criteria, or there might be a consideration of the criteria employed by the markers. From such a consideration there might then emerge the fact that the first marker has concerns about the presentation of student work and has marked the piece down on this basis, while the second has acknowledged that the work is untidy, but feels that academically it is sound. The second has marked on the quality of the content. Such a discrepancy might easily occur in assessment tasks such as portfolios, where presentation can be an issue that is wisely exploited by perceptive students.

The scenario above is not an unusual one. It illustrates some reasons why we might have stalled on the writing of assessment criteria in higher education. This and other reasons are summarized below:

- Lack of initial agreement about the features that are desirable in a piece of academic work.
- Academic autonomy and pride. There is a tendency in higher education to feel that one has a right to individual ways to judge quality in a piece of work. In the research dimension of academic life this is now changing, with the increased use of peer assessment of the quality of work.
- There are issues such as presentation and the quality of writing that do seem particularly to be subject to disagreement among teaching staff.
- There tends to be a pervading resistance to assessment criteria. This is summed up in 'I know a good piece of work when I see it', an attitude that indicates a lack of comprehension of many issues in higher education today and of the rights of a student.
- There is sometimes a difficulty in deciding how detailed an assessment criterion should be, and lack of understanding about this point can be a further reason why the use of assessment

criteria is rejected. At its most detailed extreme, assessment criteria will detract from the challenge of the task for a student, as they will tell a student what to do to gain high marks (see below).

There are more subtle reasons why assessment criteria are not used. As with learning outcomes, making learning and the requirements of learning more transparent can expose difficult issues. This is exemplified in a subject like English, where it is a characteristic of the discipline that different lecturers will take different stances towards the same subject matter. For most academic purposes, these differing constructs are part of the richness and diversity of the discipline. Lecturers expound their views in their own modules, and this is the manner in which English is taught in that module. However, if second marking occurs, the second markers may not follow the same views as the marker for whose module the work has been done. In situations such as this there may be large discrepancies and no possibility of agreement. While averaging may occur as a means of expediency, it is not appropriate. If the lecturer in charge of the module writes assessment criteria and gives them to the students and the second markers, the situation can to some extent be alleviated, even though it may open up the larger differences between the theoretical stances of staff.

The issue of precision

I indicated above that there is a concern about learning becoming too prescriptive in writing assessment criteria. This seems to occur particularly when the processes of writing learning outcomes and assessment criteria are formalized, and empty boxes are designed in a tabular form to be filled in. There may be a dictate that each learning outcome should be followed by several assessment criteria. There is a danger then that the criteria are mechanistic and that something at the heart of higher education is becoming lost for teachers and students. There is a sense that we become ruled by paperwork and administration.

Sometimes precise detail is more appropriate in writing some assessment criteria than in others. When students are in a vocational situation, and have to show evidence of their ability to tackle practical procedures before they achieve licence to practise, great precision is appropriate. On the other hand, level 3 students writing an essay should probably not be told, through the assessment criteria, exactly what content will acquire marks or allow a 'pass'. It is a matter of a teacher's judgement as to what detail in criteria will make them fair but not so informative as to detract from the challenge of the task. The stress here is on the teacher, and not the administrator. Learning outcomes and assessment criteria can 'tidy up' learning in a manner that can please administration but detract from the real learning experience (Moon, 2000).

Also relevant here is the same case that applies to the writing of learning outcomes. As the section below will indicate, one type of assessment criterion is located at the pass/fail point in assessment. It does not affect at all the learning that is above that point, and the argument that such threshold assessment criteria can liberate learning can apply in a similar manner. However, another kind of assessment criterion defines what learners should do to achieve particular marks. Using grade assessment criteria may require more sensitivity as to the degree of prescription that is inherent in the statements.

There are concerns sometimes that providing too much information about what features of work will be credited will mean that all learners work to the minimum. This is probably not the case. The well motivated and interested student will be willing to learn more than the minimum, and the poorly motivated student would probably have done less work in any situation. There are many ways to write assessment criteria, and they can be approached in a much more flexible manner than learning outcomes (see below). With levels and learning outcomes, we attempt to reach greater precision but with assessment criteria, sometimes it will be a matter of ensuring that the quality of learning is not destroyed by too much precision in assessment criteria. We seek an informed balance.

Definitions of assessment criteria

We suggested above that there are different types of assessment criteria. Two types are distinguished by the different jobs that they do in relation to learning outcomes. The third is 'the rest': other kinds of assessment criteria that are less well defined and in terms of locating standards, are correspondingly less useful. We focus initially on the first two types only.

An assessment criterion, in general terms, is a statement that prescribes with greater precision than a learning outcome, the quality of performance that will show that the student has reached a particular standard. The standard may be the threshold that is described by the learning outcome or the standard that is required in order to gain a particular grade. These differences reflect first the straight-forward use of learning outcomes, and then use of learning outcomes with the addition of a grading system. We use the terms 'threshold assessment criteria' and 'grade assessment criteria'. The definitions are as follows:

> Threshold assessment criterion: a standard of performance that a learner must reach in order to demonstrate the achievement of a specified element of learning, ie the threshold standard.

> Grade assessment criterion: a specified standard of performance that the learner must reach in order to be allocated a particular grade within a hierarchy of grades. In this case there is likely to be a series of grade assessment criteria related to the different grades.

Both of these meanings are in common use in higher education, though on the whole the difference has not been distinguished by application of the different terms. Threshold assessment criteria determine threshold standards that are relevant to learning outcomes. Grade criteria enable the allocation of a grade for the work. They indicate how well learning has been achieved above or below the threshold assessment criterion. As with learning outcomes, a threshold assessment criterion (ie that better defines the standard of the learning outcome) is equivalent to the grade criterion that represents the pass/fail point in a sequence of grade criteria. These relate grades to demonstrable performance.

For a credit system or for basic use in quality assurance, it is only the threshold criteria that are of importance. These indicate whether or not a student has reached the standard to attain a pass for a module, and whether or not she has gained the credit that will build towards the qualification. However, grading students on how well they have passed a module is a widespread practice that most students seem to favour, even if staff would sometimes be happy to mark on the basis of pass or fail. Grading can be said to provide some incentive for students to achieve above the learning outcome, and a reward for so doing.

Writing assessment criteria

Assessment criteria are generally simpler in their format than learning outcomes, and more varied in their format. In either type of assessment criterion, there needs to be either some sort of statement of what the learner will do, or a reference to the quality of the work that will be evident in the task in order to meet the criteria for success in the task. The criteria might, for example, refer to something that must be present or absent (presence of correct grammar or absence of spelling mistakes) or some role that must be fulfilled ('the report will accurately describe the processes of preparation for the task, the task itself and the outcomes'). They may be presented in a tabular form, or as bullet points, but whatever manner is chosen must provide as clear as possible an indication of the criteria. There are examples later in this chapter.

In discussing writing learning outcomes, we said that it is important to introduce tentative language such as 'the student is expected to...' because it is not possible to make a student learn. In the case of assessment criteria it is appropriate to use 'the student will...', because the student will only pass the threshold line, or gain a particular mark if she has fulfilled the criterion. In other words, the language does not need to be tentative. It is setting criteria.

The relationship between the two types of assessment criteria and learning outcomes

The main point in writing assessment criteria is that they should test, assess or relate to the learning that is mentioned in the learning outcome. An example is given of a learning outcome in the intro- ductory section of this chapter. The learning outcome says that readers will be able to 'produce' learning outcomes. 'Produce' implies that they may be written or oral, and this is useful in deciding the kind of task that is appropriate for testing the learning. It would not be technically appropriate to put the word 'write' in the outcome statement, and then to test the learning orally. It is often useful to write learning outcomes in ways that allow there to be alternative approaches to assessment.

In relating assessment criteria to the learning outcome, the main link is likely to be between the assessment criterion and the third component of the learning outcome statement. This part of the learning outcome statement indicates the quality of the learner's performance that is required in order to show that the learning has been achieved. This principle applies in a straightforward manner to threshold assessment criteria. In terms of grade assessment criteria, the learning outcome statement will provide an indication of the quality of work on the pass–fail line. It might thereby hint at the qualities of work that will gain greater marks than the threshold. However if, as we have suggested, learning outcomes are simply concerned with the location of the pass/fail point, then grade assessment criteria can legitimately bring different qualities into the picture. In a sense, this implies the existence of desirable learning outcomes, even if they have not actually been written. We consider these issues in more detail later in the chapter.

On the basis that threshold assessment criteria represent a more detailed description of a learning outcome, there will usually be an arrangement of one or more (usually more) threshold assessment criteria per learning outcome. However it is appropriate for several, or all, of the learning outcomes in a module to be tested in one assessment task, such as an essay.

In the case of grade assessment criteria, the relationship between learning outcomes and the criteria is less clear. We have said that there are some who would religiously provide a set of grade criteria for every learning outcome. This may well be a mistaken move, in that learning outcomes relate to grading only at the pass/fail point, and as we have said above, grade assessment criteria may follow the direction of the learning outcome, but will 'go beyond it' in the nature of learning prescribed. The relationship between grade assessment criteria and learning outcomes should be overt at the pass/fail point, but thereafter can be separate. It is even possible that several learning outcomes may relate to the grade assessment criteria at the pass/fail point. The key to the design of assessment criteria in relation to learning outcomes is clarity and transparency, based on an understanding of the relationships between these descriptions of learning.

Although they need to match the learning implied by the learning outcome, assessment criteria can be developed broadly from the learning outcome statement or from the assessment task. In practice, people write assessment criteria in either way, and the choice seems to be based on the nature of the assessment task, on the nature of the learning outcome statements, and on the type of assessment criteria that are being written. Sometimes it is possible for the standard of performance that indicates achievement of a learning outcome to be so clearly indicated in the learning outcome that articulation of assessment criteria is redundant. An example of a learning outcome that provides such detail is:

Example 4: learning outcome:

At the end of the module, the learner is expected to be able to perform correctly calculations on wave functions and in the solution of the Schroedinger equation for a range of one-dimensional problems.

(level 2, physics)

Figure 6.2 demonstrates how assessment criteria relate to learning outcomes.

In terms of the specificity of their language, assessment criteria could be said to lie somewhere between the description of the learning outcome statement, and the detailed activity of the task. The list of words given on pages 67 to 69 to facilitate the writing of learning outcomes can also be helpful in the writing of assessment criteria.

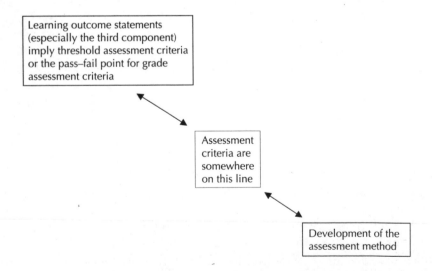

Learning outcome statements (especially the third component) imply threshold assessment criteria or the pass–fail point for grade assessment criteria

Assessment criteria are somewhere on this line

Development of the assessment method

Figure 6.2 An illustration of the relationship between assessment criteria and learning outcomes

Writing threshold assessment criteria

We indicated in the definition above that threshold assessment criteria provide more detail of what the learner will need to do to achieve the learning outcome. Where the criteria are closer in wording to the learning outcome, they are likely to be fairly generalized in reference to what the learner should do, allowing for the development of alternative assessment tasks. In this case there are likely to be relatively few assessment criteria for each learning outcome. Where the criteria are developed from the task itself, they are likely to be more detailed, defining the expected activities of the learner in more practical terms and providing a system that allows for greater precision about performance. The differences in threshold assessment criteria that might result from the two forms of development are demonstrated in the example in the box on pages 89 to 90.

Example of threshold assessment criteria

This example is worked from the basis of a sample learning outcome statement.

Example 8: learning outcome level 1, from module on skills in academic writing

> At the end of this module, the student will be expected to be able to explain and demonstrate the main features of effective academic essay at level 1.

The assessment task might be to write an essay, and a generalized threshold standard assessment criterion that is developed from, and is close to, the learning outcome might be:

> The essay will be word-processed and between 1,500 and 2,000 words on a given topic. The essay will relate to its title, will be clearly written and structured, and will demonstrate the contribution of further reading and thinking. The student will be able to explain how the essay demonstrates these features and how they contribute to its overall effectiveness.

More detailed threshold assessment criteria that are developed from the task might be:

The essay will demonstrate an appropriate working knowledge of word processing for production of level 1 written work, including layout and spell-check, as follows:

- grammar and spelling will be accurate;
- there will be reference to at least seven relevant books/papers;
- these will be correctly referenced in the recommended manner;
- there will be some evidence of analysis of ideas;
- there will be some demonstration of synthesis of ideas at least in a summary and conclusion;
- there will be an appropriate structure with evidence of introduction, development and conclusion.

In addition, in an oral session, with reference to his/her essay, the student will discuss the features of an essay that make it effective, and will show how these features work towards the effectiveness of the essay.

The assessment criteria in the example say what must be present in the essay for it to be judged to be acceptable. Since all of the statements are written at threshold, all should be reached in order for the learner to have achieved the learning outcome.

There are many formats for assessment criteria, and some are more appropriate than others. One alternative format for threshold assessment criteria is the provision of a list of features of a piece of work, and the criterion for acceptability is the presence of a given number of the features. This format is more suitable where knowledge of subject matter is required. The learner might have to mention seven out of ten topics on a list, for example, to demonstrate adequacy of basic knowledge at threshold standard. Technically in this case the actual assessment criterion is then the mention of seven out of ten and not the content of the list.

Writing grade assessment criteria

Grade assessment criteria provide a scaling of how well learners achieve above the threshold. We have characterized this in practice as provision of an incentive for learners to achieve at a higher standard than the minimum. We have said that these criteria relate to the standard set in the learning outcome only in so far as the grade assessment criterion that is at the pass–fail point must coincide with the learning outcome (or with the threshold assessment criterion that is an elaboration of the learning outcome).

We have also suggested that it may be appropriate for a set of assessment criteria to relate to more than one learning outcome. This is acceptable so long as the pass–fail point is represented by all of the learning outcomes in such a way that it is possible to identify a successful or unsuccessful student performance. The learning outcomes may indicate the 'direction' of the learning that is described in the criteria for grades above the learning outcomes, but since the latter are written at threshold, there does not have to be a strong relationship. We have suggested that it may be helpful for students and other staff to write and communicate 'desirable learning outcomes' that do relate to the grading system that is used.

Using desirable or aspirational statements to guide the writing of grade assessment criteria

For two reasons – for marketing and as a guide to writing grade assessment criteria – there is a rationale for writing desirable learning outcomes. These indicate the kind of work that might be expected from a student who is achieving at a high level. The disadvantage of writing such learning outcomes is that they tend to 'tie' down expectations of learning (see Chapter 5) instead of recognizing that real quality in higher education learning might arise from unexpected creative responses. However, maintaining the notion that they are 'desirable' and not mandatory – that they give direction rather than dictate – is a safeguard, which correspondingly allows some leeway in the writing of grade assessment criteria.

In order to maintain coherence in module development, it is appropriate to write desirable learning outcomes as a development from the usual (threshold) learning outcomes. An example is given in the box on page 92.

Example of grade assessment criteria

Example 15 learning outcome: level 1 introduction to acting/drama programme

> At the end of the module, the student will be expected to be able to work with others in small task-orientated groups, participating and interacting in the group in a productive manner for him/herself and for the group as a whole.

This learning outcome, according to the definition of learning outcome statements given in the last chapter, is written at threshold. An example of a desirable learning outcome that could guide the writing of grade assessment criteria is:

> The high-achieving learner will be able to work with and to lead others in small task-orientated groups, participating and interacting in the group in a productive manner for him/ herself and for the group as a whole. S/he will be aware of his/her role in the group, and be able to describe his/her strategies and actions.

Grade assessment criteria will now be guided by both the learning outcome that provides the pass–fail point information and the desirable learning outcome that indicates the qualities of better performance that will attain a higher grade. The assessment criteria might be:

> Fail: the learner cannot or does not participate or does not work towards helpful co-operation in a group situation.

> Average pass: the learner works with others in a task-oriented group, participates and interacts in a productive manner for her/himself and the group.

> High average: the learner works well with others in a task-oriented group, participating and interacting in a very helpful manner that suggests an increasing awareness of his/her role in the group and an increasing orientation towards the taking of leadership roles when appropriate.

> Excellent: the learner is able to lead and to act as a participant in a task-orientated group, is aware of his/her role in the group and is able to describe strategies and actions.

Figure 6.3 reproduces the basic model of module development in an adjusted form that takes account of the presence of grade assessment criteria.

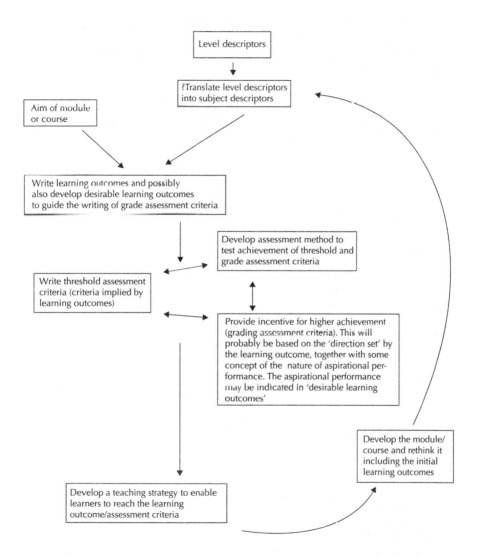

Figure 6.3 The basic model of module/course development taking into account grading criteria

Weighting assessment criteria

A system of weighting may be superimposed in many assessment situations. However, in the case of threshold assessment criteria, it is not the criteria that are weighted, but the components of the task, achievement of which indicates whether or not the assessment criteria have been reached. This means that some features of the work are identified as contributing to a greater extent to the achievement of threshold. Because grade assessment criteria are not tied in the same way to a learning outcome, a system of weighting would be expressed appropriately within the assessment criteria. Any weighting in threshold assessment criteria may be reflected in the learning outcome.

An example of weighting added to assessment criteria is in the following learning outcome:

Example 14: learning outcome:

At the end of the module, it is intended that the student will be able to write a concise, clear and tidy report of a laboratory practical that must be laid out in the prescribed format.

(level 1 introduction to chemistry module)

The assessment task in this case is likely to be the writing of one or more reports that are assessed. There is some recognition in the writing of the learning outcome that conciseness, clarity and tidiness are judgements that are more subjective than the use or lack of use of a prescribed format.

A set of threshold assessment criteria based on the assessment of three reports might be:

- The reports are to be concise.
- They are to be clearly written so that the procedures could be repeated by another on the basis of the writing.
- They are to conform sufficiently well to the prescribed format. The attainment of this criterion takes priority over the others.

In other words, the conciseness, clarity and tidiness of the report will not be considered if the format is not correct.

If grade assessment criteria are developed, weighting is easier and may be done in different ways. The following might be one form of grade assessment criteria for the learning outcome above. It is important to notice that even where weighting is a part of the development of the grade assessment criteria, the conditions set by the learning outcome all have to be achieved successfully.

Grade D, Fail: The report is not in the correct format, and is insufficiently concise, clear or tidy.

Grade C, Pass: The report is in the correct format, and is sufficiently concise, clear and tidy.

Grade B: The report is in the correct format. It is concisely written in a tidy manner with a very clear style.

Grade A: The report is in the correct format, concisely written in a tidy manner. The clarity of the style of writing is exceptional and sophisticated. It would be worthy of a level 2 student.

Another form of weighting is to allocate different marks to aspects of the same learning outcome, although it might be easier to write several learning outcomes here. Again using the previous example, weighted grade assessment criteria might be as follows. It is important to notice that this method below represents a different way of allocating marks.

To achieve the learning outcome, the report must reach a minimum standard in the use of the correct format, the conciseness and clarity of the writing and the tidiness of the report (40% of the mark).

Above this, up to 10% more can be given for concise writing.

Up to 10% more can be given for clarity of the writing.

Up to 5% more can be given for the overall tidiness of the presentation.

Up to 35% more can be given for the skilled and excellent use of the prescribed format.

The way in which the marks have been allocated here is analytic as opposed to holistic. In analytic marking, the marks are allocated to individual criteria or individual characteristics of the work. In holistic marking, marks are allocated on the basis of overall judgement of all or several criteria, as in the example above (Gosling and Moon, 2001).

More generalized forms of assessment criteria

As I indicated at the start of this chapter, there is a third group of assessment criteria. These are in addition to those that describe the threshold performance, giving more details about the learning that will achieve the learning outcome, and the grade assessment criteria that indicate the quality of work needed to gain a particular grade. We suggested that this third group broadly represents 'the rest': other assessment criteria that do not fit the first two groups. However, in more specific terms, these are usually the criteria that are more generalized, and that do not relate to any specific curriculum or to specific learning outcomes. Examples of this form of assessment criteria are provided at the end of the box on pages 98 to 105.

One form of these generalized assessment criteria that is in very common use in institutions deals with grading. It specifies the qualities of student performance that will merit a particular grade (or grade range), so it will be presented as a sequence of criteria. The sequence may be designed to be associated with a particular kind of task: in other words, it may be designed to describe the different qualities of essays. However, it may be written in sufficiently general language to be associable with a wide range of assessment tasks: such as project work, examination responses, essays and oral work.

Sometimes such a form of criteria is written to describe performance at a particular level in higher education, but often the same set of criteria will be used for two or more levels in student progression. For example, the degree classification system is often used for grading purposes throughout a programme, with very general descriptions of performance associated with it. To be allocated as a first, a piece of work is likely to be described in something like the following kinds of terms:

> Outstanding work: extremely able and accurate execution, going beyond the set requirements of the task, demonstrating wide reading which is effectively assimilated into the work.

Such a description may also be used for application to a laboratory report or an essay or a dissertation at any level. There are, however, some problems associated with this commonly used system. The first problem is that the criteria are not associated with learning outcomes. It is a system that is detached completely, and the nature of grading may not even indicate where the pass–fail point is. For example, where degree classification terminology is used, where is the pass–fail point? Is it at a third, or is it between a lower second and a third? How does such grading relate to learning outcomes?

A second problem more specifically relates to the degree classification system, but is caused by the confused thinking around the use of generalized assessment criteria. Staff have been known to say that they cannot allocate firsts to level 2 students in that these students 'just don't know enough yet'. Such a view indicates that the work of level 2 students is being judged in relation to the criteria for final degree classification and not to the level in which students are working at the time. Such ideas need to be clear in a well-ordered assessment system. In a well-ordered assessment system, the grades relate to established learning outcomes at a well defined pass–fail point.

Another problem with the generalized form of grade assessment criteria which are applied for a range of assessment tasks is imprecision. How much do the criteria really tell a student about the standards of work that will gain a particular grade in any particular assessment task? To what extent can they enable consistency between markers? Varied interpretation of such criteria can allow for considerable subjectivity. This problem is particularly apparent in descriptors that are lists of words or phrases that are applied to a task without explanation of the quality required for pass–fail or for gaining grades. For example, students might be told that a piece of work should display:

- critical thinking;
- originality;
- development of argument;
- evidence to support conclusions;
- the use of reference material;
- an adequate conclusion.

Such a set of general assessment criteria provides some guidance to the student as to what qualities in a piece of work will be valued, but then it probably describes what would be valued in any piece of academic work. It does not really indicate how well a student must do to pass or fail. Such criteria do not ensure either that several markers will be using the criteria in the same way for the allocation of marks, without perhaps further discussion with student work in front of them. The development of this approach by the addition of a range of quality indicators may help markers, and it may help the students to understand why a mark has been attributed, but without further statements, it still does not relate to standards. An example of such ranges is:

80 +	exceptional
70–79	excellent;
60–69	very good;
50–59	satisfactory;
40–49	just pass – but weak;
below 40	very weak or poor work.

The student does not know what weights a marker might attribute to the ideas given in the list, and may not fully understand what, for example, 'critical thinking' might look like in a piece of work.

Examples of assessment criteria

Most of the examples below follow on from learning outcomes used to illustrate Chapter 5. They are numbered in the same way. Those not represented here may have been developed within the earlier sections of this chapter or have not been used for illustrative purposes in this chapter. Both threshold and grade assessment criteria are illustrated in different formats. In some cases the assessment criteria have been developed from the task, and in other cases the criteria have been developed directly from the learning outcome, and the choice of task to test the criteria remains flexible. After the illustrations of threshold and grade assessment criteria, there are several examples of generalized assessment criteria that are not associated with particular learning outcomes.

Examples of threshold and grade assessment criteria

Example 2 learning outcome: level 2 BEd programme

(b) At the end of the module the learner is expected to be able to, within the context of a class situation, demonstrate and evaluate the use of appropriate examples of positive reinforcement for the purpose of the improvement of behaviour.

Assessment method:

in the context of three teaching sessions, observed by her mentor, the student will demonstrate three examples of positive reinforcement in the class situation as a means of encouraging improvement of behaviour.

Threshold assessment criteria:

- The learner will demonstrate at least three examples of positive reinforcement in order to improve behaviour.
- The examples will show that the learner understands the principles of positive reinforcement.
- They will be appropriate to the context and situation within the classroom at the time.
- The learner will be able adequately to evaluate the effectiveness of her own actions and the consequences of it, recognizing any obvious ways of improving her practice.

Example 4 learning outcome: level 2 physics

At the end of the module, the learner is expected to be able to perform correctly calculations on wave functions and in the solution of the Schroedinger equation for a range of one-dimensional problems.

Assessment method:

the learner will perform calculations on wave functions and calculations in the solution of the Schroedinger equation for one-dimensional problems, showing in a detailed manner, the ways in which they have achieved their results.

Grade assessment criteria:

Grade range below 40: failure to solve the calculations. No method given or completely incorrect method.

Grade range 40–49: calculation incorrect; the learners will show evidence of ability to make the calculations correctly but the demonstration of how the calculation was done is poor, incoherent or not sufficiently detailed.

Grade range 50–59: the learners will show evidence of the ability to make the calculations correctly but the demonstration of how it was done mediocre.

Grade range 60–69: the learners will show evidence of the ability to make the calculations correctly. The demonstration of how it was done is good, coherent and reasonably detailed. There is evidence of considerable understanding of the methods involved.

Grade range 70+: the learners will show evidence of the ability to make the calculations correctly; the demonstration of how it was done is excellent, coherent, detailed and very well explained, showing great command and understanding of the methods involved.

Example 6 learning outcome: level 3 mathematics

At the end of the module, the student will be expected to be sufficiently familiar with the techniques of multivariate analysis in order to be able to handle straightforward multivariate data sets in practice.

Assessment criteria are derived from the learning outcome, hence method not yet developed.

Threshold assessment criterion:

The students will demonstrate the ability to handle straightforward multivariate data sets in a practical situation.

Example 9 learning outcome: use of a learning outcome to alert students to potential plagiarism (based on Gosling and Moon, 2001) – could be in any discipline, probably in a skills module level 1

At the end of the period of learning, it is intended that the student will be able to discuss how plagiarism can occur intentionally or unintentionally in academic work, and identify ways of avoiding it through appropriate referencing.

Assessment method:

a) A question in the short answer paper to be done in class on the meaning of plagiarism in the academic context.
b) In the coursework essay for the module, marks will be given for correct referencing.

Threshold assessment criteria:

a) Correct identification and brief discussion of the means by which plagiarism can occur intentionally or unintentionally in academic work.

b) Correct referencing in at least five references in the coursework essay, using the appropriate system and methods as demonstrated in class.

(Comment: in this case, the learning outcome is tested in two separate assessment tasks. This is entirely appropriate and can be a useful technique for the testing of skills learning outcomes where the skill underpins other work that may be assessed for its contents or other characteristics.)

Example 11 learning outcome: Master's level, reproductive health

At the end of the module, learners will be expected to be able to appraise the consequences of a range of key socio-cultural influences on sexual and reproductive health (including sexually transmitted diseases, adolescent sexuality, female genital mutilation, the effects of culture and media).

Assessment method:

assessment criteria derived from the learning outcome, and no specific task is identified. The task could be an unseen question in an examination or an essay question.

Grade assessment criteria:

Fail: the work produced in response to a relevant question suggests that the learner is not able to perform the process of appraisal, eg cannot adequately show the consequences of the influences mentioned; does not sufficiently demonstrate understanding of the influences mentioned in the learning outcome; does not identify sufficient or adequately, the nature of the influences. There is no evidence of knowledge even to the extent of that discussed in the lecture, or the question is not answered.

Third: the work identifies some of the socio-cultural influences, suggests some understanding of their effect on sexual and reproductive health, but the treatment of the topic is superficial and/or not discussed in sufficient breadth. There is no evidence of knowledge further than that covered in the lecture.

Second: the treatment of the question is adequate. The learner identifies and discusses at least the socio-cultural influences mentioned in the learning outcome. The work discussion demonstrates useful understanding of the influences and their action on sexual and reproductive health, is of sufficient depth and breadth and demonstrates some reading around the topic in addition to the material recommended.

First: as the description of the criterion for the Second, but there is evidence of reading and thought around the topic that goes well beyond that discussed in the lecture or in the recommended reading.

Example 12 learning outcome: Master's level, learning log module in a leadership programme

At the end of the module, in an oral presentation, making reference to their learning journal entries, learners will be expected to evaluate the role of reflection in their work situations, indicating its values and the role or potential role of negative influences. They will be able to indicate how they can improve their use of learning journals in future use.

Assessment method:

an oral presentation for 15 minutes in front of peers and a tutor, all of whom will judge the quality of the presentation against a series of questions on its quality. The individual questions will be judged to be passed if they are ticked by at least all but two of the peers. The tutor will count up responses.

(Comment: peer assessment is to be used here. Learners are to be assessed as 'adequate' or 'not yet adequate'. Those who are judged to be 'not yet adequate' will be expected to repeat the presentation at a later stage in their programme.)

Assessment criterion – the real criterion is that at least five out of seven potential passes on questions will indicate 'adequate', and two or more 'not passed' will constitute 'not yet adequate'. The means of judging whether the criterion has been reached posed as questions:

In the presentation does the learner evaluate the role of reflection in the work situation in a considered manner?	Yes No
Do the illustrations read from the learning journal represent good examples of reflection in the work situation?	Yes No
Does the evaluation indicate the values of reflection?	Yes No
Does the evaluation appropriately discuss negative influences?	Yes No
Has the presenter considered how the learning journal can be used in a future situation?	Yes No

Are new methods of using the learning journal mentioned, ie methods that are different from current practice?   Yes No

Is the whole presentation coherent and well considered (as opposed to incoherent and superficial, showing little thought)?   Yes No

Example 13 learning outcome: level 1 skills in physics

At the end of the module, students will be able to demonstrate effective grasp of a range of communication skills that will underpin their further studies in physics. These will include maintenance of a physics note-book, preparation of a CV, the ability to read an academic article and discuss it in a brief presentation.

(Comment: it could be argued that example 13 represents more than one learning outcome. By having all the communication skills in one outcome, the implication is that a student failing one part, fails the whole learning outcome. It can be assumed that there will be other learning outcomes for this module, that also represent a number of small tasks.)

Assessment method:

during the two semesters of this module, there are various situations in which students are asked (without forewarning) either to perform these tasks (compile a CV in the manner that has been demonstrated; read a paper and discuss it in a brief session, or hand in the notebook that will have been maintained during laboratory work).

(Comment on assessment criteria: in this case, a little like the previous example, threshold assessment criteria and grade assessment criteria are combined to provide a simple grading system.)

Threshold assessment criteria:

The physics notebook will be neat, accurate and will describe at least two simple physics investigations as a good basis for writing a more formal report.

The CV will be presented in a tidy, well-ordered and informative manner, and be of the quality that could be sent to a potential employer when job-hunting.

The discussion of the article will demonstrate that the article has been read and understood. The discussion will be intelligible and concise, providing an adequate summary of the content of the article and a reasonable conclusion.

Grade assessment criteria:

All of the tasks must be performed adequately for the learner to be seen as passing the learning outcome. If one task is not adequate or not handed in at the appropriate time, the student will be deemed to have failed to achieve the learning outcome.

If the tasks are performed adequately, the student will be awarded a 'pass'.

If two or more of the tasks are judged to have been performed in an above average manner, the student will be awarded a merit.

Examples of generalized assessment criteria

The criteria below are not associated with any particular learning outcome.

Criteria for a postgraduate award

This is more like a marking scheme, but counts as assessment criteria since it does attempt to describe the qualities of work itself.

70% or more: Excellent. The work will be of very high standard and will reflect knowledge and autonomous development of reasoning processing well beyond that given in class or in standard works. There is clear evidence of depth and breadth in reading.

60–69%: Very good work which is well developed beyond that given; demonstrates sound knowledge and reasoning; depth and breadth of reading.

50–59%: Average. The work is reasonably competent, though there may be some weaknesses. Knowledge is adequate and while it demonstrates reading beyond the class or in standard works, it might be patchy or not broad.

40–49%: Compensatable fail. There is knowledge of core material but the knowledge and the processing of knowledge is weak or limited. There is only little evidence of wider reading.

39% and below: Fail. The work does not reach the standards in

Master's level level descriptors. There is no evidence of further reading or considered thought about the subject matter.

'Criteria' for an oral presentation

The list below is the kind of list that students might be given as 'assessment criteria' for an oral presentation. This list does not really qualify to be termed 'criteria' since there is no means of telling whether a student has performed satisfactorily or unsatisfactorily on each requirement. Only a few examples are provided here. In Chapter 8 on assessment, a more complete list is provided.

Clarity of ideas in the presentation.

Clarity of speech.

Quality of argument.

Qualify of introduction.

Quality of conclusion.

Eye contact with the audience.

Use of overhead slides or Power Point.

Management of questions, etc.

The vocabulary of assessment criteria and learning outcomes: a tale of dubious interpretation

This brief section is relevant to both Chapters on learning outcomes and this chapter on assessment criteria. It picks up an issue that has been raised on several occasions: that words are slippery and defining some learning performances with any kind of precision can be very difficult. We have used the word 'wordplay'. We return again to this issue here, because it becomes more serious when it is applied to assessment criteria. Precise and common understanding for vocabulary matters more in assessment criteria, because a student can pass or fail a module on the basis of the comprehension of a word.

The thinking here is based on a matter that comes up time and again in courses on working at Master's level. There are several words that are commonly associated with Master's degree functioning, the meaning of which is usually varied in interpretation across a group. A particularly important example is 'critical analysis'. Students are often told that good quality work at Master's level will show evidence of critical analysis. However, a group of experienced lecturers often will not be able to provide an agreed or common definition of 'critical analysis'. If they do attempt to define the phrase, they may either suggest that it means that the underpinnings for an idea are analysed to see if the idea is substantiated, or they will say that it means that the idea is critically compared and contrasted with other parallel ideas. It is interesting to think about how students might define such terms when they are rarely defined and discussed, but merely given as if everyone understands the meaning.

7 Assessment methods and teaching strategy

Introduction

If the map of module development (which is repeated as Figure 7.1) were to be followed in a clinical manner, the chapters on assessment method and teaching strategy would be separated. The chapter on assessment methods would provide a list of methods that would enable the setting of assessment criteria that would, in

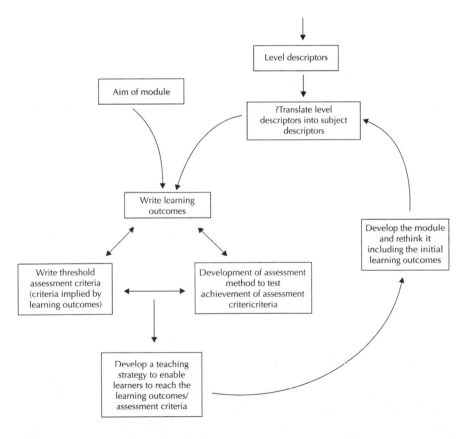

Figure 7.1 Basic map of module development

turn, allow judgement of whether learning outcomes had been attained. On the basis that assessment criteria have also been discussed as a means of establishing a grading system, we would also consider aspects of assessment methods that allow a judgement of how well the learning has occurred above the minimum. The chapter on teaching strategy would consider how best to teach and manage student learning so that the learning outcomes and requirements for grades could be achieved. In practice, however, the choice of assessment method is determined by teaching issues as well as the bare essentials of assessment. For example, it is often the assessment procedure (criteria and method used) that will drive the student's learning. In addition teaching strategies are usually concerned with the broader development of learning than that specified only in module learning outcomes. This might be stated in terms of the development of the whole person, or in terms of development of the student within the discipline. There are many techniques in pedagogical situations that exist for the dual purposes of improving learning and enabling the process of assessment to occur. For example, an essay may be a means of testing assessment criteria, but it is also a powerful means of encouraging students to broaden their knowledge and understanding, to validate existing ideas and to explore in and around a particular topic. To consider assessment separately with concerns only for the stated learning outcomes is simply too clinical a view of higher education as it is in practice. Taking this more general stance is, in effect, a recognition that the learning on a programme is more than the sum of the statements of anticipated learning outcome. It is not, however, to suggest that the statement and assessment of learning outcomes is without value in its own right as a process to underpin standards.

This chapter does not attempt to go into great detail about assessment and teaching, but picks out important points that are sometimes missed in more detailed texts or those focused more thoroughly on assessment methods. In the first part of the chapter, we consider these wider purposes of assessment in relation to learning and teaching. In the second part, we move on to consider the relationship of assessment to the quality of learning. This relationship should be considered in the development of assessment methods, and also it informs the relationship of level descriptors to their expression in learning outcomes.

The wider role of assessment

On a threshold or quality assurance model of module development, the role of the assessment method is to provide a medium for the development. In turn the assessment criteria will enable the judgement of whether or not learning outcomes have been achieved (see Figure 7.1), and possibly the means of grading work.

On the basis of the statement above we can say that the minimum requirement of an assessment method that is used for formative assessment is that it should provide the means of testing learning outcomes through development of appropriate assessment criteria. Most assessment methods will enable the testing, in some way, of most learning outcomes once we go beyond insensible situations such as trying to test literary understanding through the provision of calculations to solve. Creative thinking has its place. It is not, for example, uncommon to come across the desire to ease the pressure of marking assessment tasks by the use of computer-marked multiple choice questions. While it is possible to test learning outcomes that involve complex cognitive processing through such questions, it may be difficult to test more general understanding as opposed to specific ideas. In this case, for example, the use of complex case study material, given separately as a basis for questioning, can be helpful.

So what is assessment for, beyond the provision of a medium for appropriate assessment criteria for quality assurance and grading purposes? Some purposes are related to the provision of feedback, but we should consider feedback both to teacher and learner.

Assessment procedures provide feedback:

- for the learner on her learning;
- to the teacher on the learning of the learners;
- to the teacher on her teaching;
- on issues of the quality of the course in general.

Feedback in itself enables both teacher and learners to modify their behaviours within the activities of both teaching and learning, but it has other consequences. Feedback from assessment may enable learners to *make decisions about future choices in learning*: other modules that might be followed, for example. Assessment procedures may also have a role in *indicating when the learner is ready for progression to, for example, a more advanced course.*

Sometimes the rationale for assessment will only be to provide feedback (formative assessment), although this should still relate to the module learning outcomes. If the assessment session is half way through a module, learners may not have reached the ability to achieve the learning outcomes, or they may achieve some only. Lastly, the feedback that comes from assessment *enables course or module organizers to make decisions about the future organization of modules*, courses and so on.

In reality the provision of feedback from assessment is often not as helpful as it might be. The requirement of assessment methods to test the achievement of learning outcomes implies that they are implemented at the end of a course or module. However, that is too late for feedback to be useful to the learner. By the time results are available, the student is often engaged with other modules and in situations that may make earlier feedback seem to be fairly irrel-evant. This is one of the pitfalls of a modular system in which learning is assessed and apparently then can be 'left behind'. Earlier formative assessment is required in order to ensure that feedback is useful. It may be the case that we do not take sufficient advantage of classroom tests which may be peer marked as a means of providing feedback to both learners and teachers (Angelo and Cross, 1990).

Another factor that encourages the placing of assessment at the end of modules is that *it encourages learners to continue to attend* to the end of the teaching input. Like the other conflicts that concern the timing of assessment procedures which are mentioned above, this problem can be circumvented by splitting the assessment procedure into several parts that serve different purposes, or some marks may be allocated for attendance.

Another purpose for assessment tasks is to *test that learners can put ideas learned in one modality into another*. The most common example would be where students told how to operate a practical procedure are then tested and assessed on the demonstration that they can perform the procedure itself, or a sample of the procedure.

The major reason for using assessment, however, encompasses all of the purposes above: it is that *assessment motivates or drives or encourages learning*. We could also say that it may steer learning, and mean that in a negative sense: it is now widely recognized that students' learning is increasingly determined by what they know of the assessment procedures that they are likely to encounter. At one time it was assumed that learning was driven by passion for and interest in the subject matter, and perhaps more often this was the case when only around 5 per cent of the population went into higher education. However, if the reality is different now, we must take account of it, and assessment methods need to be considered in relation to the type of learning that they require of the students. It is worth bearing in mind also that it is not a matter of actually what the assessment procedure is that will determine or steer learning, but what a student perceives it to be (Moon, 1999a).

If we are cynical for a moment, there is a further set of purposes for assessment that are encapsulated in the statements that 'we assess students because we have always done it', 'because students expect it', and 'because that is what higher education does'. These statements represent the situation in many areas of higher education: that assessment is a procedure that is isolated and seen as an activity in its own right without links to learning outcomes, assessment criteria, levels of learning and learning itself. It is just an activity of higher education. We should be aware of the purposes that we intend any given assessment method to fulfil, and design it appropriately with all of the purposes in mind.

Some ideas that underpin the development of assessment methods

This section summarizes some ideas already mentioned, adds more and applies them in the context of the choice or design of assessment methods.

There is a balance to be struck in assessment issues between the educational merit of the procedure, and the time and effort that is involved for staff and students. The process of getting the balance of assessment right in terms of time and effort expended is an important issue for staff and for students. In recent times, the introduction of learning outcomes in an unconsidered manner has often led into situations in which students feel that they are over-assessed, and, at the same time, staff are stretched by too much marking. Sometimes this is because there is an attempt to use a separate assessment procedure for each learning outcome, rather than using an assessment method that tests several outcomes at a time. Sometimes it is because there is an unmovable belief that every learning outcome must be assessed. I have suggested that in reality, there may be a process of sampling learning outcomes for assessment (see Chapter 5).

Sometimes the situation of over-assessment arises because institutional regulations have instructed that modules must be of a uniform and a particularly short length. This will be alongside the usual regulation that every module must be assessed at the end of the module. There may also be a dictate on the word length of examinations or word length of essays. Such a set of regulations leads almost inevitably to a situation in which students face perpetual assessment tasks, and staff face perpetual marking. In such cases there may be a desperate attempt to sort out the situation by changing assessment methods, when some of the fault lies with the regulations. For example, modularization does not always mean that assessment must be timed at the end of the taught module. Though it will usually suit students to be assessed directly after the teaching has occurred, there are good educational arguments for delaying assessment so that the process of revision can allow for reconsideration of the material in the light of subsequent learning, or simply the passage of time for further thought. When we always assess directly after the teaching has occurred, those with good memories for the content of lectures can benefit. Good learning is that which is considered and thought through in relation to wider ideas.

In addition, modularization does not necessarily mean that every module must be of a uniform length or 'shape'. Allowing some modules to be larger, spanning for example two semesters or more, reduces the load of assessment and provides for greater integration of learning. In terms of the 'shape' of modules, too, there are good educational arguments for 'long thin' modules that span a period of time, but with less frequent teaching. Such modules allow for the picking up of topical matters and then relating them to ongoing learning.

Getting the balance right between teaching or contract time and assessment requires considerable thinking if we take into account the various purposes for assessment and the role it can play in directing and encouraging learning. An additional consideration is that since assessment tasks play a significant part in the enhancement of learning, their existence may be well justified on the basis of promoting good learning. What is required then may be an explanation to students that some forms of assessment are a part of the encouragement and shaping of their learning, and not – or not only – about the allocation of grades or marks. Unfortunately, such an explanation does not deal well with two issues. The first is the marking burden for staff, and the second is the unfortunate fact that many students are strategically minded enough not to bother about tasks that will not contribute to their eventual module grades (Kneale, 1997).

One approach to the marking burden issue for staff is through setting up self and/or peer assessment situations which, in themselves, enhance learning (see later in this chapter). The second issue may be dealt with by allocating a few module marks to assessment tasks which have the purpose of enhancing learning. Alternatively we could employ an injunction that we perhaps do not use sufficiently: that is making the completion of a formative assessment task a condition of passing the module. The task is not allocated marks as such, but feedback is given. Such matters can be encompassed in the statements of learning outcomes, and sharing the outcomes with students can be an important means of justifying the approach taken.

An assessment method does not test the learning itself, but a representation of the learning. We have mentioned before that this is an important and basic principle. The process of learning is different from the process of representing that learning (Moon, 1999a). There are a number of corollaries of this statement. First, students may be better at learning than at representing that learning, perhaps because the stress of assessment conditions modifies their potential performance, or they may be more able in one form of assessment than another. In addition, if learners learn from assessment procedures, or if they adopt a strategy of learning in accordance with their expectations of the procedure, then different assessment tasks can have a significant effect on the kinds and qualities of learning that occur (Eisner, 1991; Moon, 2001b)

Assessment may concern the process or the product. This is best explained with reference to an example. Sometimes we are interested in the product of learning from a laboratory experiment. On another occasion, the interest may be in the ability of a student to write up the experiment in a format that is appropriate, and then we are expressing interest in the process. In many situations there may be interest in both the process and the product, but perhaps with weighting towards one or the other. Learning outcomes and assessment criteria should make clear the basis of interest. The issue is particularly of relevance when we discuss the assessment of reflective activities later in this chapter (Moon, 1999a).

Subjectivity is likely to creep into assessment processes. We are human. It is hard not to be influenced by what we read on an essay in front of us, liking or disliking views expressed in relation to our own considerations. Even with the best written assessment criteria, it is difficult to circumvent subjectivity in complex material. Second marking is one solution, but that brings its own problems, as exemplified in the case of disciplines where different conceptions of the same subject matter are celebrated – until it comes to agreeing about the approach taken by a student. English has been mentioned as an example of such a discipline.

Assessment needs to be monitored for its validity and reliability. Validity in assessment is present when the task tests what it purports to test. An examination is not a valid assessment tool when it tests a student's ability to cope with examination conditions rather than her attainment of the learning outcomes for the module. On the basis that assessment tasks test the representation of learning and not the learning itself, this principle further supports the notion that learning outcomes and assessment criteria should be written in terminology that reflects the manner in which the learning will be represented, not just the learning itself. In other words, it is not just knowing something that is important, but the ability to explain it orally (in an oral test), describe it in writing (in a written test) and so on.

There are several forms of reliability in assessment. One form requires that several assessors will come to the same conclusion about the work (as reaching the threshold, or attaining a particular mark). Another form of reliability requires that the decision about a piece of work should be the same when it is considered after a time lapse has occurred.

Assessment tasks may be boring for students to perform and for staff to mark. Seeing assessment as a source of boredom is a symptom of the attitudes expressed earlier in this chapter, that assessment is a process that occurs because it is what is expected in higher education. Paying consideration to the manner in which assessment relates to learning outcomes and assessment criteria and other purposes that it serves is a start to change. There are many methods of assessing that are more interesting to staff and students than methods currently employed. They can be short (where a short form of assessment is desirable), and effectively challenging of learning. Not sufficient use is made of short answer questions, for example, perhaps given in class situations. Short questions to be answered on half a page can be much more challenging to learners than long questions to be explored or 'wandered around' or bluffed over several thousand words, and the need to deal with material in a succinct manner is more appropriate to the world of employment.

There is a balance to be struck also in the explicitness of the assessment criteria, in terms of enabling students to know what it is that is going to be tested, and in provision of a reasonable test of whether that learning achieves or does not achieve the learning outcomes. This is a technical issue: the balance does need to be struck, and assessment criteria should not degrade the level of challenge faced by the learner in achieving learning outcomes. It is a matter of practice, discussion and learning from experience what formats and level of detail are appropriate for different disciplines and their traditional (and non-traditional!) forms of assessment.

Assessment drives learning: the implications for assessment and teaching strategy

I shall say more about this point because it is so important for the manner in which modules are constructed. It is a matter that relates to every element in the map of module development and, indeed, supports the sequence that is depicted on the map. If assessment drives learning, then we have to be clear about the kind of learning that we want from students before we choose assessment methods. On the map (Figure 7.1), the description of the learning that is required of students is represented in the level descriptors that inform the writing of learning outcomes. This section, therefore, takes us back to levels and will aim to enhance understanding of levels by discussion of two models of learning. These models make particular sense of the way in which learning and progression in learning is described in level descriptors. More detail on these discussions of learning and many more references are presented in Moon, 1999a and 2001b.

The role of choice of approach to learning

In staff development workshops, when staff are asked to brain-storm what they mean by 'a good learner', typically they suggest ideas such as the following:

- can concentrate;
- good time-keeping;
- tries to understand for herself;
- makes an effort;
- challenges;
- takes risks;
- gets work in on time;
- asks questions;
- writes clearly;
- is interested;
- is motivated;
- turns up for class;
- is an active learner;
- is organized;
- relates what she is learning to current knowledge;
- thinks, and so on.

When they are asked for the characteristics of 'a poor learner', they might say:

- seems not to be interested;
- is not strategic;
- does not try to understand;
- is quiet;
- is a passive learner;
- is vague;
- does not seem to be enthusiastic;
- cannot manage well;
- tries to find ways of not working hard;
- is not motivated;
- is unsure about her learning, and so on.

These 'off the cuff' conceptions of good and poor learners accord very well with the outcomes of work done on approaches to learning (Marton, Hounsell and Entwistle, 1997; Trigwell and Prosser, 1999).

The work on approaches to learning stemmed from research on learning that began in Sweden in the 1970s. Instead of looking for the influences on the quality of learning within the environment of learning, or the nature of instruction or instruction materials, researchers began to ask the learners about the approach that they were adopting for a learning task. Typically a learning task would be the reading of a short piece of text, with an assessment task of answering questions on the text afterwards. In terms of the approach that was adopted, it was found that some learners were attempting to understand what the writer was trying to 'get at' in the piece, whereas others were learning the facts mentioned: sometimes in detail, but without trying to understand the meaning.

The terminology adopted at a later stage for these approaches to learning was 'deep' and 'surface' approaches. In terms of the assessment tasks, generally those who took a deep approach were more successful, unless the assessment task simply focused on facts. There are a number of determinants of the approaches adopted: for example, guesswork about the assessment task, habits in learning and the understanding of learning processes. For some people, the idea of learning concerns the learning of facts. Also, however, the learners were influenced in their approach by their anticipation of the demands of the assessment task.

A generalized description of a learner who takes a deep approach to learning includes the idea that the learner endeavours to understand the meaning of the material of learning, the ideas that underpin it, and she relates these ideas to what she 'knows' from previous learning experiences. In contrast, the taking of a surface approach implies that a learner tries to learn the facts without trying to understand the ideas that underpin the facts. In this way, such a learner is not likely to be able effectively to relate the learning to previous understandings.

Because surface learning is an insecure form of learning, with much reliance on memory rather than understanding, taking a surface approach to learning tends to generate anxiety, and anxiety tends to perpetuate a more superficial approach to learning in itself (Entwistle and Entwistle, 1992). Students may start a semester with intentions to take a deep approach to their studies, but as assessment tasks pile up and their social life and/or part-time work demand energy, their approach to learning may tend to change. It would appear that most higher education students are actually capable of taking a deep approach to their learning, but for a number of reasons will not necessarily adopt it.

The story, however, does not quite end here. Further research indicated that a third approach to learning tasks might be described. Some students managed well in assessment tasks despite what appeared to be a fairly superficial approach and not a particularly interested attitude. They were the well organized students who took trouble to find out as much as possible about learning outcomes, assessment criteria and assessment methods, and learned and performed as was necessary to fulfil the requirements. This was labeled the 'strategic' approach. Such an approach is characterized by the effort on the part of the learner to know as much about the conditions of learning and assessment as possible, so that she can tailor her learning efforts in such a way as to get the maximum mark for the minimum effort. Some would suggest that being strategic about learning is not an approach in the same way as the deep and surface approaches, but is a further quality that influences the choice of approach for a given task.

Learners certainly need to be strategic, particularly when they are managing part-time work and a reasonable standard of social life alongside engagement in higher education learning. Indeed, being strategic about learning is a quality that an employer would applaud. Going back to the brainstormed lists of attributes of good and poor learners earlier in this section, it is interesting to note that good learners reveal elements of a strategic approach combined with a deep approach. What makes poor learners poor is, in part, a lack of strategy and personal organization.

The notion of strategy brings us back to the learner's perception of the learning task. Taking a deep approach to learning will only bring about success if the learning task actually tests meaningful learning – and this is the case with many, but not all higher education assessment tasks. We can maximize the chance that students will adopt a deep approach to learning if they perceive that the learning that will achieve the best result is meaningful learning. The expectation of meaningful learning is reasonably well documented in the level descriptors, but understanding of the notion of different approaches to learning will help in the translation of the descriptions of level requirements into the writing of informative and appropriate learning outcomes.

Development of understanding of knowledge

Another set of ideas that seems usefully to underpin the way in which learning is presented in level descriptors was investigated in several projects in the last 30 years (Perry, 1970; Belenky *et al*, 1986; King and Kitchener, 1994). The ideas relate to the way in which learners conceive of the construction of knowledge itself, and it is primarily in the higher levels of higher education that this work has relevance (particularly at Master's level). King and Kitchener's work on what they called 'reflective judgement' is the broadest in remit as well as the most detailed. They worked with both genders and a range of ages in empirical studies that lasted over 15 years.

In their work on reflective judgement, King and Kitchener used subjects' capacity to work on what the project team called 'ill-structured' problems as an indicator of how subjects considered knowledge and how they used it in solving problems for which there was no definite answer. Ethical issues provide a good example of such problems. They tested subjects' concepts of knowledge and their processes of justification for responses that they produced in problem solving situations. Such issues in reasoning are particularly tested in the cognitive skills of the manipulation of knowledge in the higher levels of higher education: such as analysis, evaluation and argument.

King and Kitchener identified seven stages of development towards reflective judgement, and what is considered as true reflective judgement is seen as existing only at the most advanced two stages. An important point to note is not only the existence of the stages, but that people who are at different stages in their ability to work with uncertain knowledge may well coexist in the same stage of education. They may therefore conceive of the same material in different manners. One of Perry's books captured the significance of this in a title, *Different Worlds in the Same Classroom*. The characteristics of the stages are summarized in the box on page 120. The last two or three stages only should be relevant to higher education, though Stage 7 may not, according to the writers, be achieved by (American) undergraduates.

Stages of the understanding of knowledge reflected in the stages of development towards reflective judgement (King and Kitchener, 1994)

In the *pre-reflective stages (1, 2 and 3)*, people do not acknowledge that there is the possibility that knowledge can be uncertain and because of this, they cannot understand that there can exist problems that do not have a correct solution. This means that they do not need to seek reasons or evidence for the solution to a problem. These stages are characteristic mainly of young children, who start to move beyond them when the complexity of such issues as religion confront them, or when they recognize that those that they consider as authorities pose differing views.

In the *quasi reflective thinking stages (4 and 5)*, there is an acknowledgement that some problems are ill structured and that there may be situations of uncertain knowledge. While those at this stage do provide evidence for their reasoning, they do not know how to use it appropriately. In the earlier stage, while all individuals are seen as having a right to their own opinion, the reasoning of others who disagree with them must be wrong. Later there is recognition that there are different forms of evidence, and that different frames of reference rely on different forms of evidence. However, there is lack of understanding that evidence needs to be compared and contrasted and that frames of reference can be compared and contrasted.

There are two *stages of reflective judgement (6 and 7)*. In these stages people understand that knowledge is not given but constructed and that 'claims of knowledge are to be understood in relation to the context in which they were generated' (King and Kitchener, 1994). This implies further that a response to an ill-structured problem in one time might be different at another time. In the earlier stage of reflective judgement, there is a tendency to develop judgements on the basis of internal considerations. In the most sophisticated stage, intelligence is reflected as a skilled and sensitive ability to work with the complexities of a situation, with imagination that is used in the proposition of new possibilities and hypotheses. There is a willingness to learn from experience.

There are many influences at the present time that will tend to reduce the challenge of learning so that the standards of learning as reflected in the level descriptors are not upheld. The increase in numbers in higher education has been mentioned, but a related matter is the importance for institutions to retain students once they have been admitted. There is probably a tendency to hold on to students who are not really capable of maintaining the standards required for a programme. It is in the relationship of assessment to level learning, as described in the level descriptors, that the key to upholding standards exists. There are many other conceptual models of learning that relate closely to the progression depicted in level descriptors, but the two presented in this section seem to be particularly apt.

8 Specific techniques and methods in assessment

Introduction

This chapter consists of relatively short sections of useful information to support procedures that are related to assessment. Most of the procedures described contribute to student learning to a substantial extent.

The sections in this chapter are:

- Peer and self assessment.
- Developing assessment criteria with students for tutor, self or peer assessment.
- Assessing students in groups.
- Assessing processes in academic work: oral presentations.
- Assessing processes in academic work: reflective writing or learning journals.

Peer and self assessment

We mentioned peer or self assessment as a way of gaining the benefits for learning in an assessment procedure without necessarily involving extra marking for staff. Self or peer assessment is a process in which students are put into the role of assessors of their own or of each other's work (Race, 1991; Boud, 1995). The method may be used for any assessment task, not only, as is often thought, group assessment. It may involve the attribution of marks, formative comment or both. There is potential for variation in the level of responsibility that students have in the process and in the significance of the marks or comments that they attribute. At the one extreme students may be ticking items on a pre-prepared protocol, or at the other extreme and far more valuably, they may be developing assessment criteria along the lines of the stated learning outcomes as well as marking. In terms of the significance of the marking, their assessment, to a greater or lesser extent, may be monitored and potentially over-ruled by tutor marking, and self or peer marked material may be the whole or a small proportion of a marked piece of work.

Some of the reasons for using self/peer assessment are as follows.

- Self/peer-group assessment may save time for staff. It can take a while to set up, and time is needed for the management of it, but time might be saved once it is running. Time will be taken with each new group of students in teaching them to self/peer assess. The likelihood of saving of time is not sufficiently definite for it reasonably to constitute the sole reason for adopting a peer and self assessment system: improving student learning is a more reliable rationale.
- Self/peer assessment is a learning experience for students. They learn more about:
  - the process of assessment and the responsibility of the assessor;
  - working with learning outcomes and assessment criteria;
  - what is expected of them in their own assessed work (standards);
  - how to assess their own work – an employability skill;
  - working with the work of others. This provides them indirectly with feedback on their own work;
  - engaging as learners. Peer assessment develops involvement in learning and it should have spin-offs in other areas.
- Using peer and self assessment changes the role of students from passive to active. If there are ideas about increasing student-centred learning in the university, then this is a good starting point in the way that it involves changing orientations of staff and students towards learning.

There is often concern about the reliability in self and peer assessment. Research on self and peer assessment suggests that students are reliable as assessors of their own or others' work so long as reasonable safeguards are in place (Boud, 1995; Gibbs, 1995). Monitoring students' assessments may not take as long as full marking and may be varied in its thoroughness.

Students often do not at first like the idea of assessing their own work. A common argument is that it is the work for which staff are paid. Such arguments may be the surface expression of unease about the fairness of procedures and competitive rivalry. Once experienced in the process, however, students tend to acknowledge that they learn from the process and find that it helps their learning.

There are various issues to consider in adopting a process of peer or self assessment, for example:

- When to introduce self/peer assessment. Should it be early on in the programme or when students are more experienced as students (and – on the negative side – are more assertive about what they want and do not want)?
    - the number of marks to be attributed to peer/self assessed work;
    - the level of responsibility;
    - the level of monitoring;
    - the power of staff to overrule student marking, and so on.
- How to ensure that there is consistency in the marking across all student marked work. Unlike their teachers, students are not likely to see all of the work from the whole class, so there can be a loss of the overviewing role, unless a teacher takes this on.

Peer and self assessment can be applied in almost any area of assessment. It is very important, however that clear assessment criteria are developed and that the tutor is willing to expend time and effort in the first place, explaining the rationale for the process and basically getting it to work. This is of paramount importance. The students must know the basis on which they are attributing marks, judging pass/fail status or giving feedback, and they need the confidence in the belief that they all know and can work on this basis.

Examples of some ways in which peer and self assessment can be used are:

- Students assess colleagues on an oral presentation, either about their discipline (where content might count) or on any subject matter (in order to focus on the process of giving a presentation).
- Students assess themselves or their peers on seminar presentations.

- Self and/or peer assessment of performance occurs within a group project. In this case the interest may be in the team or group work of the whole group, the performance of the individual as a group member, or the focus might be on the product of the group's work.
- There is self and peer assessment of written work. A system of peer assessment of essays can be a good method of helping students to give feedback to each other, but equally appropriately the subject matter may be laboratory reports, short answer questions, e-mail work and other formats.
- Students assess their own or others' poster work. There are plenty of other examples.

The sections below on developing assessment criteria with students and on working with student groups are particularly relevant to this section (see also Boud and Falchikov, 1989; Gibbs, 1995; Boud, 1995; Hounsell, McCullough and Scott, 1996; Jordan, 1999; Brown and Glasner, 1999).

Developing assessment criteria with students for tutor, self or peer assessment

This method can be used to produce criteria for any method of assessment and it can have considerable benefits for students' learning and their approach to assessed tasks. It is important to bear in mind that assessment criteria must relate to the learning outcomes developed for the module. The following sequence of activities is suggested.

- Students write a list of qualities that they think are important in a piece of assessed work of the type under consideration. Depending on student numbers they might work on this individually or in small groups.
- Each individual or small group provides one or two criteria (depending on numbers) that they consider to be the most important. These are listed on a flipchart or whiteboard. There should not be overlaps between contributions, so some items listed will be from lower in the initial individual or small group lists.

- The whole group considers whether there are any areas of criteria missing (by looking at their initial lists). Missing areas are added.
- It is then a matter of bringing down the size of the list on the white-board to around 6–10 criteria for marking. Going back around the groups, in sequence each group chooses the most important criterion to the point where the 6–10 criteria have been selected. Again the final list is reviewed and any adjustments are made (eg overlaps are eliminated or close criteria are reworded or combined).
- The criteria are reworded so that they are clear and any further description is added. It is important that all of the students have a similar understanding of the meaning of the criteria.
- The tutor or the group may make the next decision. The format of the protocol for marking is likely to be one of the following:
  - a list of criteria with space for marks (eg out of 10);
  - a list of criteria with columns (for ticks) or symbols (to be circled etc) indicating the quality of the performance, eg from 'poor – needs help here' to 'excellent';
  - if the criteria are threshold criteria, then 'pass' or 'not pass' will need to be entered against each criterion, or a means developed whereby the decision can emerge from the results obtained, or space for comments may be left against each criterion (with or without other space for grading).
- On the actual form, there needs to be space for a total mark if appropriate and perhaps space for general comment, identification of strengths or weaknesses or areas for improvement etc.

(This exercise is broadly based on material in Brown and Dove, 1991.)

Assessing students in groups

As well as the economy in time for staff, there are educational justifications for setting tasks for groups to perform together. These are likely to be mentioned in the learning outcome for the module. However, some design issues need to be considered. For example, it can be difficult to differentiate between those students who contribute more and those who contribute less to the outcome, and this can be a problem for the students as well as the assessor in terms of perceptions of fair treatment. A collection of suggestions for overcoming this problem is listed below. Some of the methods of overcoming the problem of differentiating workload employ group work skills that are valuable in their own right. Where the group itself does some of the assessment, there is further value in helping the group to develop its own assessment criteria (see above). It will be noted that the different methods may actually be assessing different elements of the work or weighting them differently. The relevant learning outcomes may determine the most appropriate methods to pursue.

The material below is derived from a number of sources including Brown and Knight (1994) and Race (1991).

- All in a group are assigned the same mark.
- The group task is broken into subtasks for individuals and the subtasks are marked separately. The feasibility of this depends on the divisibility of the task. It can lead to rather separate pieces of work and little actual teamwork.
- The total mark is given to the group, and the group members then split up the mark according to the amount and quality of work done by individuals. This should probably imply that the group members are asked to set up some assessment criteria on which their judgement can be made (see above). The assessment criteria will relate to contributions made to the outcome of the project or to the functioning of the group. Any difficulties are sorted out by viva.
- A basic mark is allocated to all group members, and then the group allocates to each member an additional (smaller) mark for contribution. The comments above are relevant. The assessment criteria will relate to contributions made to the outcome of the project or to the functioning of the group. Any difficulties are sorted out by viva.
- A more sophisticated form of the two arrangements above can occur where different roles are allocated to group members. The assessment criteria for individual contributions (whether a whole or part of the mark) relate to the roles taken (eg performance in the collection of data, in a co-ordinator role and so on).
- A basic mark is allocated to all members, and a smaller mark awarded on top of this for individual presentations or other individual contributions.
- The same mark is allocated to the entire group, but there is then a question given on the topic of the group work (eg in an examination).

- 50 per cent of the mark is allocated to the group work and a further 50 per cent of the mark is allocated on the basis of an oral interview of individuals.
- Marks are allocated entirely by individual orals.

The problem of those who do not contribute fairly to group work can be tempered at the start of the work by encouraging learners to choose with whom they should work. The known lazy learners will usually not be chosen. Another way is to ask all participants to sign the work before it is submitted. (Those who have not contributed may not be there to sign.) A slightly more refined version of this method is to ask the whole group to list the others within their group who have contributed. They will usually not list those who have not contributed.

Support materials may be developed to help students in their assessment processes. These might be completed after each group meeting or at dedicated sessions with the tutor in attendance. Issues discussed can relate to the monitoring of personal contributions. Students might be asked to comment on their attendance at meetings, their general involvement in the group and how they have contributed to the thinking and research processes. They might also be asked to consider more complex group behaviours such as their support for and encouragement of others in the group.

If a focus or the focus of the project, as determined in the learning outcome, is the group work behaviour of students, it will be necessary to develop assessment criteria. As with oral presentations, there will need to be consideration of what actual features of behaviour should be developed into assessment criteria. Some assessable features of behaviour in team or group functioning are as follows. The student:

- is engaged in the group and with the group;
- can show qualities of leadership;
- is able to provide direction for group activity (eg project planning);
- is involved in the execution of the project work;
- can play a supporting role of others in group activity;
- can suggest solutions for issues within the context of the group's work;
- is involved in the presentation of the group's work;

■ demonstrates interest in the maintenance of the group functioning as well as the project.

Assessing processes in academic work: oral presentations

Some topics are difficult to assess. The difficult areas tend to be where we are attempting to assess processes or skills: most academics are able to cope with written or number work that is relevant to their disciplines. Below I provide lists of features of behaviour from which assessment criteria may be developed. I present in the lists far more features than would ever be used for any piece of assessed work. A tutor or students working in peer or self assessment could not manage to assess on all of these variables. This is particularly the case in any form of performance such as a presentation, where there is no permanent record of the work and the assessor must bear in mind all of the criteria as she watches the performance. The learning outcomes for the module, and any other purposes for the assessment, will determine which criteria will be valued for any piece of work.

Some assessable features of behaviour in oral presentations are as follows. They are deliberately displayed in a variety of forms.

■ Does the content relate to the title and or purpose of the presentation?
■ Is the breadth of the content sufficient?
■ Is the depth of the content sufficient?
■ Is the message clear?
■ Is the argument consistent?
■ Is sufficient evidence given to support arguments?
■ Is there evidence of appropriate critical thinking?
■ Are conclusions drawn appropriately?
■ Is the focus sharp?
■ Does the presenter put her own point of view?
■ Is the class engaged; is their attention maintained?
■ Is the response to questions and comment competent?
■ Organization and management:
   – timekeeping;
   – management of questions or comment;
   – general management of whole presentation.

- Presentation:
  - audibility;
  - clarity of articulation;
  - presence;
  - posture, eye contact etc.
  - management of notes or props;
  - pace;
- Use of resources (quality, fitness for purpose etc):
  - overhead transparencies;
  - handouts;
  - use of board or flipchart etc;
  - use of other resources.
- Overall structure:
  - coherent approach, appropriate structure;
  - clear identity of beginning (summary), middle and end (conclusion);
  - well 'signposted' structure.
- Creativity:
  - use of imagination in content or presentation;
  - originality.

Assessing processes in academic work: reflective writing or learning journals

Increasingly often students are being asked to reflect, to write reflectively or to write a learning journal in their work in higher education. The idea is usually put forward in the context of the enhancement of learning or the development of professional skills. It would be unusual if reflective work was seen mainly as a tool for assessment. Often the preference of staff would be that such work would not actually be assessed and in an ideal world, students would do it because they wanted to enhance their own learning. The world, however, is not ideal and the reality is that students often will not tackle work unless it is assessed and they see that they can earn marks from it.

The development of assessment criteria for reflective work is particularly difficult since often we are unsure what distinguishes reflection from other academic and 'everyday' processes (Moon, 1999b; 2000). A reasonable comment is that reflection is an encouragement for learners to follow the lines of their own thinking, to work without a curriculum. How can that be assessed or graded?

Writing a learning outcome that includes the activity of reflection may be all very well, but it is when we need detail of what will constitute evidence of performance that difficulties arise. Similarly there are no general definitions of a learning journal. A learning journal (or log, diary or notebook) is what it is until it is defined under local circumstances, related to a learning outcome or assessment criteria are written for it (Moon, 1999b; George and Cowan, 1999). Sometimes a theoretical underpinning may be present for reflective writing or learning journals, such as the experiential learning cycle (Kolb, 1984), but again, no one theoretical approach is agreed.

This vagueness about reflective or journal writing should not diminish its potential value. Much important learning can emanate from such activities (Fulwiler, 1987), but thinking, planning, monitoring and rethinking need to go into the activities when they are set.

Given that there is no agreement about appropriate criteria for marking such work, the necessary task for staff is to develop their own criteria based on the learning outcomes for the module and their awareness of any broader purposes that have justified the use of such methods of learning / assessment. Unfortunately a common scenario is as follows. Students have been asked to write a learning journal because someone thought it was a good idea, but that person is not involved in the development of the journal now. Some vague guidance was given to students about how they should write at least once a week, and how they should review the relevant activities of the week and comment on areas in which they need to learn more. They have been told that the journals will be assessed. The journals are due in next week. No one among the staff group has really considered how the journals will assessed or graded (except that a precise grade is expected for each journal). The learning outcome made reference to students learning to be reflective practitioners.

A very first task of developing reflective tasks is to consider the nature of the learning outcomes for the module or course. A second consideration is to think about how the task will be assessed at the time the task is developed, and relate the form of assessment to the purpose and anticipated outcomes of the task. Sometimes the purpose will be to develop reflective writing/reflective practice skills, and then the assessment criteria will need to concern the processes evident in the assignment. If it is the outcome of the process of reflection that is important, then the task might be an essay or an examination that tests the knowledge developed. This is no different from many more routine assessment methods, but it is an entirely appropriate manner of assessing learning that has resulted from the use of a journal or other reflective writing.

If an essay is used, students might be required to quote from their journals – and perhaps to hand in the journal alongside the essay as evidence that it was written – but the journal itself will not be graded. More often, however, where reflective activities are used with students, the learning outcomes will indicate that the ability to reflect is a focus. In other words, the process is important (sometimes as well as the product).

How then is the process of reflection to be assessed? There is a need to develop assessment criteria that can guide the work of the students in the first place and enable fair assessment later. Only general guidance can be given about assessment criteria because, as I have said, the context of the use is a local decision. Moon (1999b) provides a list of what might be termed general attributes of reflective work or journals. A list of assessment criteria can easily be developed by selecting those attributes that meet the local conditions for the work.

These somewhat superficial attributes do not touch on what might be called the 'depth' of reflection, and since much student work on reflection tends to be somewhat descriptive, criteria that relate to depth can be helpful to ensure that there is more useful learning from the work (Moon, 2001c). Hatton and Smith (1995) provide a useful framework for assessing the depth of reflective writing, but just telling students that a criterion on which they will be assessed is the relative depth of their reflective writing may not be sufficient. We suggest that if depth of reflection is an issue, students need to be introduced to this in a practical manner. Appendix 4 includes an illustrative exercise that not only introduces the idea of depth in reflective work to students, but also provides some indications of the kinds of criteria on which depth might be judged. There are a number of theoretical bases for the notion of depth (Moon, 1999a; 2001b). In particular the work of King and Kitchener (1994) that was described in Chapter 7 is of relevance.

Exercises such as this can be developed in the context of the actual student work that is to be set. Provision of illustrations of reflective work such as this gets over some of the problems that are associated with the assessment of reflective processes.

As an illustration of some criteria for a learning journal used in a PGCE (secondary) programme, see the box on pages 133 to 134. The journal had already been set by the time the criteria were developed, and hence the criteria needed to encompass reference to the original instructions. This made them somewhat more complicated than would be desirable for comfortable assessment. Some useful devices are present in the criteria. For example, for the criteria relating to presentation and multidimensionality, marks are only deducted or added where the journal was of particularly good or poor quality. This feature eases the tasks of assessment and as a principle could be applied more generally.

An illustration: criteria that underpin the description of a good journal (PGCE secondary)

1. Evidence of critical reflection that results in obvious new and usable learning:
   - a description of the 'stimulant' for reflection (eg incident, quotation, theoretical idea);
   - evidence of going back over the incident (etc), thinking about it on paper, bringing to bear relevant extra information (theory, things said, advice, previous experience etc);
   - the drawing out of some sort of conclusion which may indicate new areas for reflection or something learned;
   - evidence of learning from the reflective process that is then used in the planning or operation of further activities.
2. Evidence of reflection on teaching experiences and the process of learning to teach.
3. Evidence of reflection on the manner in which pupils (school students) learn.
4. Evidence of learning from the relating of theory to observations and practical situations with respect to any aspect of teaching and learning, with inclusion of references to other material.

---

5. Evidence of a developing self as teacher. This will be demonstrated in accumulating remarks that build towards a 'philosophy of my teaching' or of 'me as teacher', eg statements of beliefs about procedures, about values, observations that suggest an awareness of taking up a particular style or position as a teacher.
6. Presentation in an adequate format. Journals that are excellently presented will gain a few extra marks (specified). Journals that are very poorly presented will lose a few marks (specified) but a wide range of presentations will be 'adequate' with no loss or gain of marks.
7. Evidence of 'multidimensionality'. Good journals will draw from and refer to a wide range of types of material. For example, a journal that does not display multidimensionality might consider 'what I see happening in the classroom' and relate it to one or two few standard references. A journal that is multidimensional will draw from a range of texts, quotations, pictures, relevant media items and so on. Additionally, it may show evidence of the learner 'standing outside the situation' in order to observe herself. It may show evidence of understanding of there being different viewpoints about an event. The opposite to multidimensionality is likely to be a narrow journal mostly based on observation or expression of own feelings, with few references etc. As with presentation, most journals are likely to fall into a wide band of 'adequacy' in respect to multidimensionality. A few will lose marks (specified) because they are exceptionally narrow and a few journals will attract extra marks (specified) because they are exceptional in this respect.

9 The sum of the parts: some considerations on working at programme level

Introduction

The map of module development includes one last element that we have not explored. It suggests that we should review the whole module once the individual stages of development have been processed. This is an important stage for the module. It is the stage at which the elements can be tuned and fine-tuned so that their interrelationships are transparent.

We have said that any part of the map can be modified, except the agreed set of level descriptors that guide the standards of learning. Let us assume this process has been followed, and we have the module developed as a coherent unit of learning and assessment of that learning. But what have the individual modules to do with the programme, when it is a programme that will be the unit of identity to which students and their employers will relate? In the beginning of this book we were careful to indicate that the map is relevant to module or course development. In previous renditions of the map (eg Gosling and Moon, 2001), it was applied to programme development as well as module development, but the dual use has inconsistencies. We do not, for example, develop learning outcomes for a programme, but programme outcomes which are different in some important respects. There are different issues to consider now.

This chapter explores the relationship of modules to programmes. This is addressed from two specific angles, both of which themselves represent current and practical areas of considerations in higher education:

- the design and writing of programme specifications;
- multidisciplinary or modular programmes and issues of coherence.

The chapter therefore both has a very practical element and follows a more theoretical line of exploration.

The programme specification (introduced in Chapter 5) is a description of the programme that is required as part of the process of quality review in higher education (QAA, 2000b). In considering programme specifications, the focus will be on the writing of educational aims, programme outcomes and the teaching, learning and assessment methods. These are the elements of the programme specification that need to relate most closely to the module design that has been discussed throughout this book. Going back to the title of this chapter, they are the 'sum of the parts'. The writing of programme specifications has encouraged much thought about the nature of multidisciplinary or modular programmes. This is because the specifications require a statement of unity about a programme, whether it is a single honours programme or a programme in which more or less every student follows a different curriculum (QAA, 2000d). Multi-disciplinary programmes may not have been considered as other than the total of a sum of different modules. From this thinking, two important questions underpin all of the areas of discussion in this chapter.

- Should a higher education programme be the sum of its parts or more than the sum of its parts?
- If coherence is desirable in a programme, how can it be developed in other than a single honours programme?

While multidisciplinary programmes are used here as a means of illustrating issues about programme structures, it is important to note that much of what is written in this chapter can apply equally to single honours programmes. Factors that would increase the similarity are where the department is large, with many perhaps largely young or new staff, and where there is considerable choice in module selection.

Programme specifications: an overview

There are a number of detailed texts about programme specifica-tions. We do not pretend here to cover all of the issues, but just to pick out those relevant to the main subject matter of this book. Further information on programme specifications can be obtained from the QAA guidelines on programme specification (QAA, 2000b) and articles edited by Jackson (2000).

Programme specifications have been developed by the QAA to support the new review processes at subject level. To some extent the process of writing programme specifications could be seen as parallel to the process of the design of modules: a consideration of all of the separate parts to ensure that they match and provide a sense of quality and coherence. In the current deliberations about the future of review processes, it appears that it will be judicious for institutions to require the writing of programme specifications as a 'baseline' account of their educational provision, and as a basis of programme or subject self-evaluation.

It is, perhaps, the existence of the subject benchmarks and their representation within the programme specification that has stimulated much of the thinking about programmes. Or more cynically it could be said that the thinking is often more about the manner in which the programmes are described on paper. We introduced the development of the QAA subject benchmarks in Chapter 5, because they have some relevance to the writing of learning outcomes (as we said earlier). The benchmarks provide statements about what learners might be expected to have achieved when they graduate with an honours degree. In most of the benchmarking groups, there are benchmarks for 'threshold' and for 'typical' students, and sometimes for 'excellent' students, though the terminology varies, and the location of the 'threshold' – and hence its meaning – also varies. In addition, the level of specificity for benchmark statements varies. Some subject statements are very vague and some are quite specific about the content of a programme.

The relationship of benchmark statements to programme specifications arises mainly in the writing of the programme outcomes. There is an expectation that programme outcomes should in some way match the subject benchmarks. There are a number of difficulties inherent in this, and two in particular should be mentioned. The first is that only around a fifth of programmes offered in higher education are pure single honours programmes. The notion that subject benchmarks are reflected in programme specifications works properly only in single honours programmes. For many multidisciplinary programmes, it does not work either because several subjects are to be represented or because students follow a variety of subjects but graduate with the same degree title. We return to this later and in the section on multidisciplinary programmes.

The second problem is inherent in the sequence of developments. Most programmes pre-existed subject benchmarks. They had their own outcomes already determined, if not actually recognized and committed to paper. There is therefore a conflict in the writing of programme outcomes. Are they a description of what actually happens in a programme, or are they concerned with a stereotyped set of statements that represent a pretence of what happens in the programme?

In the section below, we provide some practical support for the completion of the programme specification sections on writing educational aims, programme outcomes and teaching, learning and assessment sections.

Pulling the description of programmes together in programme specifications: writing educational aims, programme outcomes and teaching, learning and assessment sections

First it should be noted that the QAA 'guidelines' for the development of programme specifications are guidelines. This means that institutions should broadly follow the sections recommended, but they may choose to customize them so the terminology can vary. It is likely, however, that all programme specifications will include aims, something that accords with programme outcomes, and something on teaching, learning and assessment. These are the areas of the construction of a programme where the relationship between modules and the whole programme is expressed. They may also be the main parts of the programme specification that are completed by academic staff who work on the programme. Much of the rest of the document can be completed in a relatively standardized manner from centrally held records. It is helpful if the programme specification can be published electronically, with these other areas tentatively completed in a standardized format for the institution. Those working on the programme who are compiling the specification can then modify or add to the standard information and write in their new information in the areas that are discussed below.

Some general points about writing programme specifications

In writing the programme specification, it is worth remembering that it is a document which is largely about the process of the programme as a means of educating students towards particular outcomes, rather than a document that gives indication of the quality of the programme in terms of standards. For example, while programme outcomes are statements of the anticipated outcomes at the end of the programme, most of the other sections, including that on teaching, learning and assessment methods, concern the methods of supporting learning and assessment throughout the whole programme towards attainment of those outcomes.

Programme specification and the representation of standards

Because the programme specification is more concerned with the process leading to outcomes, the actual representation of standards could be said to be better presented at the module level, in the learning outcomes and in their relation to level descriptors. Such an indication may be made in the section on the programme specification on 'Indicators of quality and standards (17: QAA, 2000b). Something like the following words may be useful.

> In terms of learning, quality assurance is monitored with reference to module descriptions. Module description templates indicate how the aims and levels of modules are reflected in intended learning outcomes. Learning outcomes imply assessment criteria, which are tested in appropriate assessment tasks.

Another point at which standards are represented is in the relationship of the programme outcomes to subject benchmark statements (see below). There are other points of reference that represent standards. Some subject associations produce guidelines for what honours degrees will cover and more significantly, professional bodies may indicate standards as a means of delineating licence to practice in the profession. In most cases this kind of information has been incorporated into the benchmark statements for that subject.

Incorporating benchmark information into the programme specification: some general points

The points below relate to subjects for which subject benchmark statements are written, and they relate only to honours degrees because that is the level at which benchmark statements are written. As I have said earlier, the nature of the benchmark statements for different subject groupings differs considerably in detail and in the approach to the description of the discipline.

For programmes that terminate at levels below level 3, it can be useful to take regard of the benchmark statements where the programme has defined routes of progression to honours degree level. This will be the case, for example, for Foundation degrees where potential progression needs to be identified. For a Master's programme that is presented as an advanced level of an honours degree, benchmarks are likely to be relevant as an indication of orientation of the subject matter. This will also be the case where the programme is a 'conversion' programme. Where, however, the Master's programme clearly represents the development of a specialism, references to benchmark statements are likely to be little use.

There should be reference to any relevant subject benchmark statements in the programme outcomes, and they may influence the manner in which educational aims are worded. The reference may be in direct incorporation of (relevant) actual statements, a summarized version or simply use made of the terminology. Whichever of these systems is used, it is the real programme that should be described. The programme outcomes should not be presented as a list of the published benchmark statements without further consideration. Where benchmark statements are used, it should be possible to demonstrate how they are being used in the programme at level 3, and how progression at earlier levels enables those outcomes to be achieved. It is likely to be in the lack of information about progression to the benchmarks through earlier levels that the unconsidered use of benchmarks will become evident.

Where a programme that is being described in the programme specification clearly takes an alternative approach to subject matter from that implied by the statements, QAA requests that an indication of the rationale for the alternative should be incorporated in the programme specification (QAA, 2000c).

Writing educational aims of the programme

The aim statements specify a rationale and general direction which support the design of the programme. They concern what it is as a whole that the programme is intended to achieve. They provide the flavour of the programme that is intended by the programme designers. The aim statements are written in terms of the teaching intentions, curriculum coverage or the management of the learning, and the statements should not be too abstract or over-optimistic. The anticipated fulfilment of these intentions is represented in the programme outcomes, which describe the kind of learning that should be achieved by students.

Some points to take into consideration in the writing of educational aims are:

- A useful initial statement to an educational aim might be: 'The programme is intended to...'. Words that might follow this are: provide students with; prepare students for; meet the requirements of; enable students to; develop knowledge/skills in; cover... and so on.
- There may be reference to relevant vocations, or vocational standards that the programme is intended to fulfil. There may be generalizations based on subject benchmark information (bearing in mind that subject benchmarks are – at present – written at level 3).
- The format of the aim statements may be a number of bullet points or a statement that can contain more than one sentence, but the aim section should be reasonably brief. The focus of the document is on the programme outcomes and how they are reached.
- Educational aims should not extend to more than a few well chosen sentences, and should not mention aims that cannot be clearly represented as outcomes and justified in practice.
- A checklist for the writing of educational aims: the questions below are designed to support the writing of programme aims.
  - Does the statement of educational aims start with appropriate words?
  - Is there evidence in the programme of endeavour towards everything mentioned in the aims?
  - Do the aims deal with teaching/curriculum/management of learning?

- Are they introduced with appropriate words, eg 'The programme is intended to...'?
- Are the words of the aims reasonably well grounded in what can be delivered (rather than 'wish-list' material)?
- Are the aim statements reasonably brief?

Writing programme outcomes

While educational aims are about teaching intentions, curriculum coverage and management of learning, the programme outcomes relate to the anticipated learning achievement by students at the end of the programme. Since they are 'end points' of the programme at a particular level, this needs to be taken into account in the writing of the next section on 'Teaching, learning and assessment methods'. The teaching learning and assessment methods section provides information about the whole programme that leads to the outcomes at the end of the programme. For this reason linking programme outcomes to teaching, learning and assessment methods may not be a logical procedure in the programme specification. This is in direct contrast to the process of linking levels, learning outcomes, assessment criteria, methods and the teaching strategy in the development of a module.

The section on programme outcomes in the programme specification is divided into 'subject knowledge and skills', 'core academic skills' and 'personal and key skills'. We have described why this approach can create logical problems because it is a system that is frequently used in the development of modules (Chapter 5); however, as with learning outcomes, it can be useful to distinguish the skills components of a programme. It is the decision of the subject specialist how outcome statements are divided between these categories.

It is important to note that there are clear differences in the nature of programme outcomes and learning outcomes written for modules. Programme outcomes are written for a typical or average student and they may be aspirational. They are not, therefore, always directly testable. For example, programme outcomes may evidence areas of learning that are the outcomes of the student's experience of engagement in the programme, on the basis that the whole may be greater than the sum of its parts.

A useful initial statement for programme outcomes might be:

> On completion of the programme, it is expected that the student will be able to...

This style of wording should lead the programme outcomes to be written in terms of what the student will be able to do as a result of the learning. For example, it would not be appropriate to write '... will be able to be aware of (an area of the curriculum)'. Such wording provides no indication of what the learner will be able to do to demonstrate that the learning has been achieved. In the example, the outcome will need to show the manner in which the student will demonstrate the awareness. Appropriate words will be found in the relevant level descriptors, or alternatively in the vocabulary list in Chapter 5.

One of the difficulties in writing programme outcomes is the reasonable incorporation of the various sources of information that combine to characterize the actual programme. They might include:

- information from subject associations;
- information on standards from professional bodies;
- subject benchmarks;
- guidance on standard from qualification descriptors in the Qualifications Framework;
- the actual programme as it runs.

Some other points to take into consideration in writing programme outcomes are:

- It is important that the manner in which programme outcomes are written accords with the level of the qualification or award for the programme. Information about levels is obtained from level descriptors (see Chapter 3).
- Most programme outcomes will be written in such a manner that it is broadly possible to ascertain whether the learning has been achieved.
- The writing of programme outcomes must ultimately be based on the actual programme and its actual outcomes, with the level of the qualification or award indicated in the manner in which the programme outcomes are written. This is regardless of the various other reference points that contribute to the writing of programme outcomes (see above).

- There needs to be a clear relationship between the programme outcomes and educational aims.
- Where the programme substantially differs from the subject benchmark statements, there should be some statement justifying positively the stance adopted (not a statement excusing the absence of benchmark references).
- Some suggest that simply compiling all of the learning outcomes from all of the modules in a programme should fulfil the requirement for programme outcomes. While this approach might represent a quick means of filling in this section, it is based on some assumptions that do not indicate quality in a programme. First, it implies that a programme is no more than the sum of the component modules. Second, it is based on a static and naïve view of the nature of learning that is simply cumulative. It assumes, for example, that level 1 learning stays as level 1 learning, and is not modified into more sophisticated understandings at level 2 or 3. Simply writing all of the learning outcomes from component modules does not, therefore, seem to represent an appropriate approach to writing programme outcomes. Programmes with broad student choice, could not anyway be described in this manner.

Checklist for programme outcomes

The questions below are designed to support the writing of programme outcomes.

- Do the programme outcomes reflect the level of the programme in the learning challenge implied and the use of words?
- Were programme outcomes written in association with level descriptors?
- If the programme award is at level 3, are relevant subject benchmarks included appropriately in the programme outcomes?
- If a programme at level 3 deviates significantly from relevant benchmark statements, are there justifications given for the alternative programme design?
- Are there relevant professional body or subject association expectations that should be incorporated into the programme outcomes?
- Are programme outcomes written in terms of what the learner will do in order to demonstrate his/her learning rather than in terms of what is learnt only?

- Is there a relationship between programme outcomes and educational aims?
- Are programme outcomes largely achieved by most students on the programme?
- Are programme outcomes divided into subject knowledge and skills, core academic skills, and personal and key skills?

Teaching, learning and assessment methods

This section of the programme specification, unlike the equivalent description of modules, does not bear a logically close relationship to the previous section on programme outcomes. Programme outcomes are written for the level of the award or qualification, while the section on teaching, learning and assessment apparently relates to the whole programme. The section is likely to be best represented by a list of methods of teaching and the management of learning, and a list of the methods used for assessment of student work. It is worthwhile mentioning any distinctive or innovatory approaches to any of these activities.

In order to indicate that the quality of learning is monitored in the process of assessment through the development of assessment criteria, a statement such as that below could introduce this section:

> More detailed description of the manner by which learning is related to assessment through assessment criteria in the modules that make up this programme will be found on module description templates.

Programme specification, coherence and sums of parts

The design of the programme specification does allow for the possibility for a programme to be seen to amount to more than the sum of its modules, since it does not rely directly on the learning outcomes of modules to be repeated as programme outcomes. It assumes that the learning modifies and evolves to reach the programme outcomes. The nature of this 'greater gain' may be coherence itself: an understanding of how learning in one module relates to that in another module. It may also be about being a discipline specialist and working comfortably with the language and epistemology of that discipline. Consideration of the nature of the greater gains over a whole programme is a very useful staff development activity for all of those who are working on a particular programme. Unfortunately this opportunity is often lost when one lone person is given the responsibility of writing the programme specification.

Multidisciplinary and modular programmes

While the title of this section might seem to indicate a focus only on a particular type of programme, in fact most of the content of the section applies to most programmes in higher education that have a modularized structure.

It was noted above that the requirement to write programme specifications, and more particularly programme outcomes, encourages us to think about the nature of a complete programme rather than the elements in a programme. However, how do you write programme outcomes for a multidisciplinary programme when students are following unique combinations of modules? The existence of subject benchmarks is likely further to confuse the situation if a student is following several disciplines. It will not be appropriate to write the subject benchmarks from all of the disciplines, and if several disciplines are being studied, it is highly unlikely that all of the benchmarks will be reached – or, indeed, that they will be reached at level 3. This represents a conceptual difficulty of applying levels and subject benchmarks in such situations.

One way of tackling the programme specification for multidisciplinary programmes is to focus on other than the subject matter that is being learned. There may be a rationale for the development of a multidisciplinary programme that can be used to represent a programme outcome. There are also likely to be skills that students learn in common despite their different pathways through modules (Dillon and Hodgkinson, 2000). Another approach is to use the activity of writing programme outcomes as a part of the programme itself: in other words, to ask students to look at the benchmarks for the subjects that they are studying and to identify those outcomes that they expect to meet. To increase the value of this exercise, students can be asked at the same time to evaluate their choices of modules and the process of making that choice.

Developing coherence in multidisciplinary programmes

We are already making the assumption here that a programme in higher education should be a coherent experience, not a mass of bits and pieces. Coherence is not such a problem in an integrated single honours programme where a limited, if not small, group of staff work within the same disciplinary culture and have a sense of the whole experience that they wish to generate for their students. The situation is different for students undergoing multidisciplinary or modular programmes. Their programme may be unique – no one else follows the same path – and the module teachers whom they encounter in their period of learning may be from different disciplinary cultures and may never have met each other or discussed how the learning in one module relates to the learning in another.

The fact that teaching staff on many multidisciplinary programmes do not meet is one reason why the development of coherence in a multidisciplinary programme is difficult. However, at a second look, this lack of communication may mean that there might be a lack of coherence in the teaching when, in fact, it is with the results of student learning that we should be most concerned.

Particularly significant for learning on such a programme might be not the content of the modules themselves, but the boundaries between them. The QAA benchmarking activities have demonstrated clearly that disciplines have their unique understandings of knowledge, their own cultures, and their own discourses. We expect students, with little or no guidance, to cross these substantial borders and possibly to make something of the experience of crossing them. It is also likely that few teaching staff have had the experience of multidisciplinary learning themselves. If lecturers do choose to cross disciplines, they tend to be following their own interests or the topics of their research. They will be making the transition in their own time, at their own pace, ensuring comprehension as they proceed. The chances are, too, that their experience of crossing disciplinary boundaries will be very limited compared with that of some students.

What of coherence? What is it that we might be concerned to develop as the sum that is greater than the parts of a programme? Let us review our perceptions of multidisciplinary programmes. We acknowledge that many students on such programmes actually only study a relatively small number of subjects, by choice or because of the institutional or departmental regulations, and we can comfortably accommodate them as deviants from the single discipline mode. But what of those who follow many subjects? We tend to look askance at such programmes, labelling them 'pick and mix'. However, let us suppose that we reconsider these programmes within a different frame of reference: as developing in students the capacity to be truly multidisciplinary creatures. Such students would be able to cross disciplinary boundaries, to understand that different disciplinarians see knowledge differently, and to ask questions in different disciplines through their ability quickly to adapt to new discourses. They might be the prototype of real lifelong learners.

Within the constraints of a modular framework, with no 'room' for students to gain credit for activities outside their modules, how can we help students to learn to gain the understanding and skills that have been described above? There is a range of ways of achieving this, which is underpinned by a set of guiding principles. We look first at the principles.

Some principles for developing coherence

The first principle is that coherence needs to be written large in all documentation about the programme, and understood clearly to be the anticipated outcome at least by one or more key individuals who are in contact with the students. It will probably be expressed in aims and learning outcomes for the whole programme and for some modules.

There will also need to be appropriate mechanisms to enable the development of coherence, and these will be focused on learning, much more than on the delivery of ideas through teaching. These mechanisms could be in the form of special modules, some of which are described below. Within these special modules, there will need to be incentives for students to build individual understandings of how their 'bits of learning' interrelate. Such incentives will include time, appropriately guided opportunity and a valuing of their explorations, probably through assessed work. The students are likely to need to develop good skills of reflection and the ability to write reflectively. The last principle, but perhaps the most important one, is that students need to learn early on that we view knowledge through different frames of reference according to different disciplines. In the later part of their programme they will need to come to understand the constructed nature of knowledge and other basic principles of epistemology. They will need to develop well on the dimension of reflective judgement (King and Kitchener, 1994: ch. 8). We should overlay these principles by acknowledging that there is unlikely to be one method of achieving them all, and a well considered mixture of the mechanisms below is necessary.

Some mechanisms for developing coherence

Some of the mechanisms or structures in a programme that will support these principles are widely used, but often in a 'lip-service' manner, and not in a way that truly develops multidisciplinary understanding. For example, as a means of justifying a coherent approach, it is not unusual to ask multidisciplinary students to do a project that covers more than one of their subjects, perhaps for a dissertation. However, the subject matter for such research tends rapidly to become specialized and the advantages of crossing disciplines are then limited. Related to the project work can be a cross-disciplinary independent study module in which a student studies an area of personal choice, guided by learning outcomes agreed with a tutor. Another manner of crossing disciplines is to provide modules where the subject matter is skills or something like work experience. In the latter, students may be asked to study not only their learning in the workplace, but how that learning relates to learning in the context of their discipline situations.

Closer to the notion of engendering a multidisciplinary outlook is the use of planning modules early on in a programme, in which students are required to plan and justify their choices of modules (and perhaps sort out their timetables too) for the first two levels (or more) of their programme. Such modules are more effective if they are paired with later integrative modules in which, with appropriate guidance and structure, students reflect on their progress, the development of their skills and knowledge across the whole programme. It is sometimes possible to run a 'long thin' module of this sort as a thread throughout a whole programme.

One of the most effective means by which a student on a multidisciplinary programme can become multidisciplinary in outlook is through study of one or more 'theory of knowledge' modules, similar to the model used in the International Baccalaureate programmes. In such a module, students become acquainted with the manner in which different disciplines view knowledge, thereby moving towards an understanding of the role of the knower in relation to her knowledge and the constructed nature of knowledge. In this way, students can be far more prepared, and better able to learn from the different approaches to knowledge that they will encounter in a multidisciplinary programme. Theory of knowledge subject matter might best be visited at least twice in a programme, initially guided, and later providing a basis for reflection on their programme.

Conclusion

We come to the conclusion of the book. Most of the content of the book has been concerned with the development of the modules that go to make up a programme in higher education, but in this final chapter, we have implied that a programme may have more to it than simply the constituent modules. We have implied that it might be desirable for students to go out of higher education with more than a mass of bits and pieces of learning. We have suggested that in looking at whole programmes, we should, for any student, consider the coherence of the programme not only by looking at the contents of the modules, but by considering too the barriers that are represented by disciplinary boundaries. Some of this thinking is stirred up in the consideration of how to describe a programme on a programme specification form. However, in order to write the form in a reasonable manner, some of the issues might also need to be clarified and resolved.

10 A summary of module development for reference and staff development purposes

Introduction to this chapter

This chapter adds nothing new to the book in terms of content. It is primarily designed as a means of making the book easier to use. The material contained in the book is complex and is not always what one would want to wade through in practical situations when developing modules or when working in staff development situations. Chapter 10 compiles the important points about module development, levels and level descriptors, learning outcomes and assessment criteria and their relationships to assessment processes. As this material is referenced back into the main text of the book, it can also act as a more detailed index. Sometimes the sequence of information in this chapter differs slightly from that in the main body of the book.

Programmes, modules, courses, teaching and learning

- **Programmes** are usually made up of modules. Modules are complete in themselves and are assessed, though they may be obviously related to other modules. Courses are short or relatively short periods of learning that may or may not be assessed.
- It is important to recognize that **teaching and learning are separate activities.** A teacher can ensure that she teaches, but she cannot ensure that the learner learns. Only the learner can ensure that she learns. This is an important point, for general recognition that the processes described in this book are learner-centred, and for clarity about the nature of aims and learning outcomes.
- It is helpful to consider the **development of programmes at threshold (basic) standard** as a largely separate operation from grading (attribution of marks to work).

- At some stage in any discussion of module development it is worth acknowledging that **the use of words to describe learning and learning achievement is imprecise**. We are just trying to be clearer about the processes of learning and teaching than we have been in the past. There are many anomalies. It is also important to note that many words used to describe activities in learning may have variable interpretation, for example 'critical analysis' and 'reflective practice' (see page 34).

A sequence for consideration of module development and for staff development purposes (Chapter 2, page 15)

- The sequence of developing a module or short course is also useful as a sequence for covering the material in the context of staff development. The **map of module (and course) development** (Figure 10.1 on page 153) is not necessarily the manner in which most people design curricula. They usually start with an area of curriculum that they want to develop. However, this sequence shows the interrelationships between the elements, and is therefore a checking mechanism for quality review purposes.
- The map of module development is concerned with student achievement at **threshold standard** (page 15).
- **Definitions:**
  - *Level:* an indication of the standard of difficulty of the work that a student will need to undertake in order to be deemed to have achieved the credit for the learning. We also now have qualification levels that are more relevant to programme development (see below).
  - *Level descriptors:* generic statements describing the characteristics and contexts of learning expected at each level.
  - *Aim:* indicates the general direction or orientation of a module or course in terms of its content and sometimes its context within a programme. An aim tends to be written in terms of the teaching intentions or the management of learning.
  - *Learning outcome:* what a student will know, understand or be able to do at the end of a period of learning and how that learning will be demonstrated. Learning outcomes are couched in terms of what the learner is expected to learn.

- *Assessment criteria:* statements that indicate, in more detail than learning outcomes, what the learner will need to do in order to indicate that she has achieved the learning outcomes that have been specified.
- *Assessment method:* the task that is set for learners that will enable a judgement to be made as to whether the learners can achieve the assessment criteria (and hence learning outcomes).
- *Teaching strategy:* the support that needs to be given to learners to enable them to achieve the learning outcomes. There is recognition that the learning may be achieved without the involvement of teaching.

■ In terms of the **'flow' of this sequence**, level descriptors and aim statements contribute to the writing of learning outcomes. The

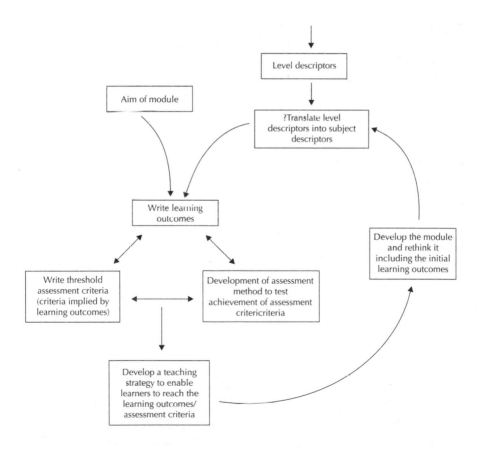

Figure 10.1   Basic map of module development

former provide an indication of standards, and the latter provide a 'sense of direction' and content. Learning outcomes imply assessment criteria. On this threshold model, the assessment method represents the development of the tasks to test assessment criteria, and teaching supports the learners towards achievement of the assessment criteria (and thereby the learning outcomes).

- When this model is used to underpin module development, it is important to ensure that there are **clear relationships between the elements**. In reviewing the process by going 'round the cycle' again any element can be modified (learning outcomes, assessment criteria etc) except the agreed level descriptors.

Levels and level descriptors (Chapter 3, page 19)

- A system of levels with associated descriptors **provides a structure to higher education**. On the basis of a recent survey, 76 per cent of institutions of higher education use a system of levels and level descriptors (page 19).
- In England, Wales and Northern Ireland **there are usually three undergraduate levels and two postgraduate levels defined.** These broadly equate to the first three years of a traditional undergraduate degree and the expected attainment of Master's students and taught doctorate postgraduate students. In Scotland, with a different system, there are often four undergraduate levels with two postgraduate levels (page 22).
- **Levels are arranged hierarchically** so that a higher level is more demanding of the learner than lower levels, and there is an assumption that higher levels subsume the learning at lower levels (page 21).
- There are **different systems** of naming and labelling levels in operation, and there are two types of systems of levels in operation in the UK now. **Credit levels** were developed to support credit accumulation and transfer systems and have become the more traditional type of level description. The newer system (2001) is the Quality Assurance Agency **qualification descriptors.** This system relates to the standard of difficulty of the work that a learner will have demonstrated in order to gain a qualification at that level. The systems are different and have different roles (page 23).

■ **The appropriate system of level descriptors to use** when considering the development of modules is credit level descriptors. When we talk of the accumulation of modules to operate as a programme that has an associated qualification, the appropriate set of descriptors is the qualification level descriptors.

■ A **comparison of the QAA qualification descriptors and the widely used SEEC credit level descriptors** indicates reasonable compatibility in terms of level implied by the descriptors (pages 25 to 29).

■ Both types of level descriptor rely on **aspects of learning** such as the complexity of knowledge and understanding, cognitive skills, key and transferable skills and sometimes more practical skills. However descriptors may be specially focused descriptors such as those used in work situations.

■ It is a useful exercise to **translate the generic terminology** of level descriptors into that of a discipline or subject. The document produced is a valuable help towards the writing of appropriate learning outcomes and assessment criteria, and the exercise is useful in staff development processes (page 46).

■ Regarding the **uses/purposes of level descriptors**, they:
  – characterize qualifications;
  – provide a structure for the design of higher education provision;
  – help to maintain standards;
  – provide structure for external articulation or accreditation of external awards;
  – provide a means of communication about higher education;
  – are used in curriculum design and development;
  – are a tool for staff development;
  – act as a tool for mapping skills and other curriculum components (Chapter 4, page 40).

■ **Hints for appropriate application of level descriptors in module development**:
  – Treat descriptors as guides, not dictates.
  – If there are inappropriate descriptions in generic descriptors, ignore them (or consider whether they should be addressed).
  – Add descriptors if there are areas of learning not addressed in the published descriptors.
  – Look at descriptors in the context of previous and later levels and other descriptors at the same level.

- Consider whether practical skills need to be developed to the same level as cognitive aspects of learning. Attributing levels to skills may not be useful (page 40).

Aims and learning outcomes (Chapter 5, page 50)

- **An example of a learning outcome** is: 'At the end of this module, the learner will be expected to be able to explain and demonstrate the main features of an effective academic essay at this level' (from a skills module at level 1).
- **Learning outcomes provide a means of describing learning** that is yet to be achieved or that has been achieved. They are couched in terms of learning. **Aims** are usually couched in terms of teaching or the management of teaching, and they can often be achieved without even the presence of a learner (page 50; 61).
- **Objectives** are written in terms both of learning and teaching (aim or learning outcome 'language') and hence are better not used for programme development purposes (page 62).
- **Some purposes of learning outcomes are:**
  - to be explicit about what is expected of a learner in terms of learning;
  - to indicate the link between learning and the assessment criteria for that learning;
  - as a means of communication about the learning to the learner or others;
  - as a tool for communication with external examiners and assessors;
  - as a means of judging consistency of volume and standards of learning within and across institutions;
  - as a means of relating actual learning to QAA benchmark statements at level 3;
  - as part of the definition of credit, contributing to the measure of volume of learning;
  - as a transcript, providing information about what a learner has achieved;
  - as a tool for mapping components in the curriculum such as skills;
  - as a tool for addressing special issues in the curriculum such as plagiarism (page 53).

- **QAA subject benchmarks** are like learning outcomes written for specific subjects at level 3 (honours degree level), though some benchmarks are not written at threshold standard (page 43).
- **The components of a well-written learning outcome** are:
  - a verb that indicates what the learner is expected to be able to do at the end of the period of learning;
  - word(s) that indicate on what or with what the learner is acting or how she will act;
  - word(s) that indicate the nature of performance that is required as evidence that the learning has been achieved.
- **They are written at threshold standard**. In other words, to pass or achieve the module, learners must achieve the learning outcomes. Learning outcomes represent essential learning.
- **Grading** is a different issue from the writing of learning outcomes. Grading is a matter of how well learning outcomes have been achieved, and may be seen as a form of incentive for the learner to achieve above threshold. The point at which grade and learning outcomes coincide is on the pass–fail line wherever that is placed.
- **Learning outcomes** must be assessable.
- **Some other points about writing learning outcomes** (page 75):
  - Most learning outcomes start with the words, 'At the end of the period of learning / module / course (etc), the learner will be expected to…'. Tentativeness is important because a teacher cannot make a learner learn.
  - Learning outcomes should be related to level.
  - They should not be too detailed. If there are more than 10 learning outcomes for a module, they will be more like assessment criteria.
  - It is possible to write learning outcomes for any kind of learning. If the learning is negotiated, then the rationale for the use of negotiated learning may be the subject matter for the outcome statement.
  - Learning outcomes for some science subjects may indicate the level through the indication of the content of the learning, where learning takes a commonly understood hierarchical sequence.

Assessment criteria (Chapter 6, page 79)

- **An example of assessment criteria:** The associated learning outcome is: 'At the end of this module, the learner will be expected to be able to explain and demonstrate the main features of an effective academic essay at this level' (from a skills module at level 1).

■ **Assessment criteria might be:**
The essay will be word-processed and between 1,500 and 2,000 words on a given topic. The essay will relate to its title, will be clearly written and structured, and will demonstrate the contribution of further reading and thinking. The student will be able to explain how the essay demonstrates these features and how they contribute to its overall effectiveness.

■ It is useful to distinguish **three types of assessment criteria** (page 84):

– A threshold assessment criterion is a standard of performance that the learner must reach in order to demonstrate the achievement of a specified element of learning, ie the threshold standard.

– A grade assessment criterion is a standard of performance that the learner must reach in order to be allocated a particular grade within a hierarchy of grades. In this case there is likely to be a series of grade assessment criteria related to the different grades.

– A generalized assessment criterion, unlike the two definitions above, does not relate to any particular curriculum or learning outcome, but may be used for different modules, sometimes at different levels in higher education.

■ **Some general points:**

– There can be a tendency to confuse assessment criteria and assessment tasks. The criteria are the bases of the judgement as to whether a learner has achieved the learning outcomes. The task is the method by which the assessment will be made (eg examination question, essay) (page 79).

– The use of assessment criteria represents a criterion-referenced system: the learner's relative success is based on her performance on the task. In a norm-referenced situation there is a predetermined distribution of gradings or passes and failures.

■ **Threshold and grade assessment criteria relate to learning outcomes.** The former are implied directly by learning outcomes and are the criteria used for basic quality assurance and credit purposes. In a system of grade assessment criteria, the relationship with learning outcomes is at the pass–fail point. It can be helpful to see the grading system as superimposed on a basic quality assurance system (page 80).

- There are many different ways of **writing assessment criteria** (page 86). They may be, for example, tabular, bullet points, written directly in association with learning outcomes or not. They describe something that should be present, or something that should not be present (eg grammatical errors). They are written in direct language because the student will only pass/get the grade if she performs as stated.
- **Assessment criteria may be developed from the learning outcome or from the assessment method** (page 88). In the latter case they are likely to be more detailed. The example in the first bullet point of this section was written from the learning outcome. More detailed threshold assessment criteria (for the same learning outcome) that are developed from the task might be:
  - The essay will demonstrate an appropriate working knowledge of word processing for production of level 1 written work, including layout and spell-check.
  - Grammar and spelling will be accurate.
  - There will be reference to at least seven relevant books/papers.
  - These will be correctly referenced in the recommended manner.
  - There will be some evidence of analysis of ideas.
  - There will be some demonstration of synthesis of ideas at least in a summary and conclusion.
  - There will be an appropriate structure with evidence of introduction, development and conclusion.
  - In addition, in an oral session, with reference to his/her essay, the student will discuss the features of an essay that make it effective, and will show how these features work towards the effectiveness of the essay.
- It may be useful to write **desirable or aspirational statements** to guide the writing of grade assessment criteria (page 91).
- A system of **weighting** may be applied to assessment situations. Here the importance of some elements of the work will be stressed in the statements of assessment criteria or, in a marking system, in the numbers of marks attributed to them (page 94).

Assessment methods and teaching strategies (Chapter 7, page 107)

■ **Assessment methods** can be regarded on the map of module development basically as a means of testing learning outcomes at threshold standard, or of allocating grades above and below the learning outcome. However, in reality there are other important purposes for assessment that have more to do with appropriate teaching strategies, and hence assessment method and teaching strategy are dealt with here together. We should not, however, forget that the basic reason for development summative assessment methods is to test the attainment of learning outcomes.

■ As assessment methods are developed, **their other purposes should be considered**. These are likely to influence the design of the method that is chosen. We should be aware of the purposes for which we are assessing, but all assessment methods will not fulfil all purposes of assessment.

■ **Purposes for assessment** include:
   - Provide feedback for the learner on her learning.
   - Provide feedback to the teacher on the learning of the learners.
   - Provide feedback to the teacher on her teaching.
   - Help students to make decisions about future choices in learning.
   - Indicate when the learner is ready for progression to, eg, a harder course.
   - Encourage learners to continue to attend classes.
   - Test that learners can put ideas learned in one modality into another (ie apply learning).
   - Motivate or drive or encourage learning.
   - 'Because we have always done it', 'Because students expect it', 'Because that is what higher education does', etc (page 109).

■ Some **ideas that underpin the development of assessment methods** (page 111):
   - There is a balance to be struck in assessment issues between the educational merit of the procedure, and the time and effort that is involved for staff and students.
   - Institutional regulations about module lengths and the timing of assessment procedures in relation to modules can cause or ease over-assessment.
   - Assessment tests not the learning, but the representation of the

learning. Sometimes students are more or less able at an assessment procedure independently of how well they have learnt the material of the module.

– It is not always necessary to attribute marks to an assessment procedure. One method of ensuring that unmarked work is at least done is to make its completion a condition of fulfilling module requirements.

– Assessment may be of a process or a product of learning, although often both are involved. Different assessment methods are implied. We should be aware of which we are testing, and this should be reflected in learning outcomes and / or assessment criteria.

– Subjectivity is likely to creep into assessment processes.

– Assessment should be monitored for its validity and reliability.

– Assessment tasks may be boring for students to perform and for staff to mark. Some creative thinking can alleviate this problem.

– There is a balance to be struck also in the explicitness of the assessment criteria, in terms of enabling students to know what it is that is going to be tested, and in provision of a reasonable test of whether that learning achieves or does not achieve the learning outcomes.

■ The notion that **assessment drives learning** has **implications** for the process of assessment. We need to be clear about the kinds of learning that we want from students, so that assessment tasks can encourage them. It is the relationship of assessment to level, as described in the level descriptors, that is the key to upholding standards. There are several helpful models of learning that inform the level descriptors and thence the patterns of learning reflected in learning outcomes, for example work on approaches to learning and on development of reflective judgement (page 115).

Appendix 1 SEEC level descriptors (revised version)

Notes on the use of the descriptors

- Areas of learning differ according to the extent to which the knowledge or skills developed are **generic** or more **subject specific**. The areas of learning are labelled accordingly.
- In general, progression is characterized by two important related factors:
  - the **autonomy** of the learner;
  - the increasing **responsibility** that is expected of the learner in the guidance given and the tasks set.
- Some or all of the following skills will be identified by subject specialists at any level. It may be useful for subject specialists to develop more detailed descriptors of these skills in association with the other level descriptors in order to determine achievement at each level.
  - investigative skills / methods of enquiry;
  - laboratory skills / fieldcraft;
  - data and information processing / IT;
  - content / textual analysis;
  - performance skills;
  - product development;
  - professional skills;
  - spatial awareness;
  - management of resources.

HE Level 1

Development of knowledge and understanding (subject specific)

The Learner:

- **Knowledge base:** has a given factual and/or conceptual knowledge base with emphasis on the nature of the field of study and appropriate terminology.

- Ethical issues: can demonstrate awareness of ethical issues in current areas of study and is able to discuss these in relation to personal beliefs and values.

Cognitive/intellectual skills (generic)

The Learner

- **Analysis:** can analyse with guidance using given classifications/principles.
- **Synthesis:** can collect and categorize ideas and information in a predictable and standard format.
- **Evaluation:** can evaluate the reliability of data using defined techniques and/or tutor guidance.
- **Application:** can apply given tools/methods accurately and carefully to a well defined problem and begin to appreciate the complexity of the issues.

Key/transferable skills (generic)

The Learner:

- **Group working:** can work effectively with others as a member of a group and meet obligations to others (for example, tutors, peers, and colleagues).
- **Learning resources**: can work within an appropriate ethos and can use and access a range of learning resources.
- **Self evaluation:** can evaluate own strengths and weakness within criteria largely set by others.
- **Management of information:** can manage information, collect appropriate data from a range of sources and undertake simple research tasks with external guidance.
- **Autonomy:** can take responsibility for own learning with appropriate support.
- **Communications:** can communicate effectively in a format appropriate to the discipline(s) and report practical procedures in a clear and concise manner.

■ **Problem solving**: can apply given tools/methods accurately and carefully to a well defined problem and begins to appreciate the complexity of the issues in the discipline.

Practical skills (subject specific)

The Learner:

■ **Application:** can operate in predictable, defined contexts that require use of a specified range of standard techniques.
■ **Autonomy in skill use:** is able to act with limited autonomy, under direction or supervision, within defined guidelines.

HE level 2

Development of knowledge and understanding (subject specific)

The Learner:

■ **Knowledge base:** has a detailed knowledge of major theories of the discipline(s) and an awareness of a variety of ideas, contexts and frameworks.
■ **Ethical issues:** is aware of the wider social and environmental implications of area(s) of study and is able to debate issues in relation to more general ethical perspectives.

Cognitive/intellectual skills (generic)

The Learner:

■ **Analysis:** can analyse a range of information with minimum guidance using given classifications/principles and can compare alternative methods and techniques for obtaining data.
■ **Synthesis:** can reformat a range of ideas and information towards a given purpose.
■ **Evaluation:** can select appropriate techniques of evaluation and can evaluate the relevance and significance of the data collected.

- Application: can identify key elements of problems and choose appropriate methods for their resolution in a considered manner.

Key/transferable skills (generic)

The Learner:

- **Group working:** can interact effectively within a team/learning group, giving and receiving information and ideas and modifying responses where appropriate.
- **Learning resources:** can manage learning using resources for the discipline. Can develop working relationships of a professional nature within the discipline(s).
- **Self evaluation:** can evaluate own strengths and weakness, challenge received opinion and develop own criteria and judgement.
- **Management of information:** can manage information. Can select appropriate data from a range of sources and develop appropriate research strategies.
- **Autonomy:** can take responsibility for own learning with minimum direction.
- **Communications:** can communicate effectively in a manner appropriate to the discipline(s) and report practical procedures in a clear and concise manner in a variety of formats.
- **Problem-solving:** can identify key areas of problems and choose appropriate tools/methods for their resolution in a considered manner.

Practical skills (subject specific)

The Learner:

- **Application of skills:** can operate in situations of varying complexity and predictability requiring application of a wide range of techniques.
- **Autonomy in skill use:** able to act with increasing autonomy, with reduced need for supervision and direction, within defined guidelines.

HE level 3

Development of knowledge and understanding (subject specific)

The Learner:

- **Knowledge base:** has a comprehensive/detailed knowledge of a major discipline(s) with areas of specialization in depth and an awareness of the provisional nature of knowledge.
- **Ethical issues:** is aware of personal responsibility and professional codes of conduct and can incorporate a critical ethical dimension into a major piece of work.

Cognitive/intellectual skills (generic)

The Learner:

- **Analysis:** can analyse new and/or abstract data and situations without guidance, using a range of techniques appropriate to the subject.
- **Synthesis:** with minimum guidance can transform abstract data and concepts towards a given purpose and can design novel solutions.
- **Evaluation:** can critically evaluate evidence to support conclusions/recommendations, reviewing its reliability, validity and significance. Can investigate contradictory information/identify reasons for contradictions.
- **Application:** is confident and flexible in identifying and defining complex problems and can apply appropriate knowledge and skills to their solution.

Key/transferable skills (generic)

The Learner:

- **Group working:** can interact effectively within a team/learning/professional group, recognize, support or be proactive in leadership, negotiate in a professional context and manage conflict.

- **Learning resources:** with minimum guidance can manage own learning using full range of resources for the discipline(s). Can work professionally within the discipline.
- **Self evaluation:** is confident in application of own criteria of judgement and can challenge received opinion and reflect on action. Can seek and make use of feedback.
- **Information management:** can select and manage information, competently undertake reasonably straight-forward research tasks with minimum guidance.
- **Autonomy:** can take responsibility for own work and can criticize it.
- **Communications:** can engage effectively in debate in a professional manner and produce detailed and coherent project reports.
- **Problem solving:** is confident and flexible in identifying and defining complex problems and the application of appropriate knowledge, tools / methods to their solution.

Practical skills (subject specific)

The Learner:

- **Application of skills:** can operate in complex and unpredictable contexts, requiring selection and application from a wide range of innovative or standard techniques.
- **Autonomy in skill use:** able to act autonomously, with minimal supervision or direction, within agreed guidelines.

Master's level

Development of knowledge and understanding

The Learner:

- **Knowledge base:** has depth and systematic understanding of knowledge in specialized / applied areas and across areas and can work with theoretical / research-based knowledge at the forefront of their academic discipline.
- **Ethical issues:** has the awareness and ability to manage the

implications of ethical dilemmas and work proactively with others to formulate solutions.

■ **Disciplinary methodologies:** has a comprehensive understanding of techniques/methodologies applicable to their own work (theory or research-based).

Cognitive and intellectual skills

The Learner:

■ **Analysis:** with critical awareness can undertake analysis of complex, incomplete or contradictory areas of knowledge communicating the outcome effectively.
■ **Synthesis:** with critical awareness, can synthesize information in a manner that may be innovative, utilizing knowledge or processes from the forefront of their discipline/practice.
■ **Evaluation:** has a level of conceptual understanding that will allow her/him critically to evaluate research, advanced scholarship and methodologies and argue alternative approaches.
■ **Application:** can demonstrate initiative and originality in problem solving. Can act autonomously in planning and implementing tasks at a professional or equivalent level, making decisions in complex and unpredictable situations.

Key/transferable skills

The Learner:

■ **Group working:** can work effectively with a group as leader or member. Can clarify task and make appropriate use of the capacities of group members. Is able to negotiate and handle conflict with confidence.
■ **Learning resources:** is able to use full range of learning resources.
■ **Self evaluation:** is reflective on own and others' functioning in order to improve practice.
■ **Management of information:** can competently undertake research tasks with minimum guidance.
■ **Autonomy:** is independent and self critical learner, guiding the

learning of others and managing own requirements for continuing professional development.

- **Communications:** can engage confidently in academic and professional communication with others, reporting on action clearly, autonomously and competently.
- **Problem solving:** has independent learning ability required for continuing professional study, making professional use of others where appropriate.

Practical skills

The Learner:

- **Application of skills:** can operate in complex and unpredictable, possibly specialized contexts, and has an overview of the issues governing good practice.
- **Autonomy in skill use:** is able to exercise initiative and personal responsibility in professional practice.
- **Technical expertise:** has technical expertise, performs smoothly with precision and effectiveness; can adapt skills and design or develop new skills or procedures for new situations.

Taught doctorate

Development of knowledge and understanding

The Learner:

- **Knowledge base:** has great depth and systematic understanding of a substantial body of knowledge. Can work with theoretical/research knowledge at the forefront of the discipline at publication-quality/peer reviewed standards.
- **Ethical issues:** can analyse and manage the implications of ethical dilemmas and work proactively with others to formulate solutions.
- **Disciplinary methodologies:** has a comprehensive understanding of techniques/methodologies applicable to the discipline (theory or research-based).

Cognitive and intellectual skills

The Learner:

- **Analysis:** with critical awareness, can undertake analysis, managing complexity, incompleteness of data or contradiction in the areas of knowledge.
- **Synthesis:** can undertake synthesis of new approaches, in a manner that can contribute to the development of methodology or understanding in that discipline or practice.
- **Evaluation:** has a level of conceptual understanding and critical capacities that will allow independent evaluation of research, advanced scholarship and methodologies. Can argue alternative approaches.
- **Application:** can act independently and with originality in problem solving, is able to lead in planning and implementing tasks at a professional or equivalent level.

Key/transferable skills

The Learner:

- **Group working**: can lead/work effectively with group. Can clarify task, managing the capacities of group members, negotiating and handling conflict with confidence.
- **Learning resources:** is able to use full range of learning resources.
- **Self evaluation:** is reflective on own and others' functioning in order to improve practice.
- **Management of information:** competently and independently can undertake innovative research tasks.
- **Autonomy:** is independent and self-critical as learner; guides and supports the learning of others and can manage own continuing professional development.
- **Communication:** can communicate complex or contentious information clearly and effectively to specialists / non-specialists, understands lack of understanding in others. Can act as a recognized and effective consultant.
- **Problem solving:** independently can continue own professional study, professionally can make use of others within/outside the discipline.

Practical skills

The Learner:

- **Application of skills:** can operate in complex and unpredictable/specialized contexts that may be at the forefront of knowledge. Has overview of the issues governing good practice.
- **Autonomy in skill use:** can act in a professional capacity for self/others, with responsibility and largely autonomous initiative in complex and unpredictable situations.
- **Technical expertise:** has technical mastery, performs smoothly with precision and effectiveness; can adapt skills and design or develop new skills/procedures for new situations.

Appendix 2   Quality Assurance Agency Qualifications Framework qualification descriptors

General C (Certificate) descriptors

Students successfully completing programme requirements at this level will have demonstrated:

(1) knowledge of the underlying concepts and principles associated with their area(s) of study, and an ability to evaluate and interpret these within the context of that area of study;
(2) an ability to present, evaluate, and interpret qualitative and quantitative data, to develop lines of argument and make sound judgements in accordance with basic theories and concepts of their subject(s) of study.

Typically, successful students at this level will be able to:

(a) evaluate the appropriateness of different approaches to solving problems related to their area(s) of study and/or work;
(b) communicate the results of their study/work accurately and reliably, and with structured and coherent arguments;
(c) undertake further training and develop new skills within a structured and managed environment;

and will have:

(d) qualities and transferable skills necessary for employment requiring the exercise of some personal responsibility.

General I (Intermediate) descriptors

Students successfully completing programme requirements at this level will have demonstrated:

(1) knowledge and critical understanding of the well-established principles of their area(s) of study, and of the way in which those principles have developed;
(2) ability to apply underlying concepts and principles outside the context in which they were first studied, including, where appropriate, the application of those principles in an employment context;
(3) knowledge of the main methods of enquiry in their subject(s), and ability to evaluate critically the appropriateness of different approaches to solving problems in the field of study;
(4) an understanding of the limits of their knowledge, and how this influences analyses and interpretations based on that knowledge.

Typically, successful students at this level will be able to:

(a) use a range of established techniques to initiate and undertake critical analysis of information, and to propose solutions to problems arising from that analysis;
(b) effectively communicate information, arguments, and analysis, in a variety of forms, to specialist and non-specialist audiences, and deploy key techniques of the discipline effectively;
(c) undertake further training, develop existing skills, and acquire new competences that will enable them to assume significant responsibility within organisations;

and will have:

(d) qualities and transferable skills necessary for employment requiring the exercise of personal responsibility and decision-making.

General H (Honours) descriptors

Students successfully completing programme requirements at this level will have demonstrated:

(1) systematic understanding of key aspects of their field of study, including acquisition of coherent and detailed knowledge, at

least some of which is at or informed by, the forefront of defined aspects of a discipline;

(2) an ability to deploy accurately established techniques of analysis and enquiry within a discipline;

(3) conceptual understanding that enables the student:
- to devise and sustain arguments, and/or to solve problems, using ideas and techniques, some of which are at the forefront of a discipline; and
- to describe and comment upon particular aspects of current research, or equivalent advanced scholarship, in the discipline;

(4) an appreciation of the uncertainty, ambiguity and limits of knowledge;

(5) the ability to manage their own learning, and to make use of scholarly reviews and primary sources (eg refereed research articles and/or original materials appropriate to the discipline).

Typically, successful students at this level will be able to:

(a) apply the methods and techniques that they have learned to review, consolidate, extend and apply their knowledge and understanding, and to initiate and carry out projects;

(b) critically evaluate arguments, assumptions, abstract concepts and data (that may be incomplete), to make judgements, and to frame appropriate questions to achieve a solution – or identify a range of solutions – to a problem;

(c) communicate information, ideas, problems, and solutions to both specialist and non-specialist audiences;

and will have:

(d) qualities and transferable skills necessary for employment requiring:
- the exercise of initiative and personal responsibility;
- decision-making in complex and unpredictable contexts; and
- the learning ability needed to undertake appropriate further training of a professional or equivalent nature.

General M (Master's) descriptors

Students successfully completing programme requirements at this level will have demonstrated:

(1) a systematic understanding of knowledge, and a critical awareness of current problems and/or new insights, much of which is at, or informed by, the forefront of their academic discipline, field of study, or area of professional practice;
(2) a comprehensive understanding of techniques applicable to their own research or advanced scholarship;
(3) originality in the application of knowledge, together with a practical understanding of how established techniques of research and enquiry are used to create and interpret knowledge in the discipline;
(4) conceptual understanding that enables the student:
   ■ to evaluate critically current research and advanced scholarship in the discipline; and
   ■ to evaluate methodologies and develop critiques of them and, where appropriate, to propose new hypotheses.

Typically, successful students at this level will be able to:

(a) deal with complex issues both systematically and creatively, make sound judgements in the absence of complete data, and communicate their conclusions clearly to specialist and non-specialist audiences;
(b) demonstrate self-direction and originality in tackling and solving problems, and act autonomously in planning and implementing tasks at a professional or equivalent level;
(c) continue to advance their knowledge and understanding, and to develop new skills to a high level;

and will have:

(d) the qualities and transferable skills necessary for employment requiring:
   ■ the exercise of initiative and personal responsibility;
   ■ decision making in complex and unpredictable situations; and
   ■ the independent learning ability required for continuing professional development.

General D (Doctoral) descriptors

Students successfully completing programme requirements at this level will have demonstrated:

(1) the creation and interpretation of new knowledge, through original research or other advanced scholarship, of a quality to satisfy peer review, extend the forefront of the discipline, and merit publication;
(2) a systematic acquisition and understanding of a substantial body of knowledge which is at the forefront of an academic discipline or area of professional practice;
(3) the general ability to conceptualise, design and implement a project for the generation of new knowledge, applications or understanding at the forefront of the discipline, and to adjust the project design in the light of unforeseen problems;
(4) a detailed understanding of applicable techniques for research and advanced academic enquiry.

Typically, successful students at this level will be able to:

(a) make informed judgements on complex issues in specialist fields, often in the absence of complete data, and be able to communicate their ideas and conclusions clearly and effectively to specialist and non-specialist audiences;
(b) continue to undertake pure and/or applied research and development at an advanced level, contributing substantially to the development of new techniques, ideas, or approaches;

and will have:

(c) the qualities and transferable skills necessary for employment requiring the exercise of personal responsibility and largely autonomous initiative in complex and unpredictable situations, in professional or equivalent environments.

Appendix 3 Differences in implied level between SEEC credit level descriptors and QAA QF qualification descriptors

This material is derived from an article published in *SEEC News*, Summer 2001 (Moon, 2001a). It considers the differences between the SEEC credit level descriptors and the QF qualification descriptors. The section below deals only with implied differences in level, not the conceptual differences which are considered in greater detail in the text of this book.

The SEEC credit level descriptors are more detailed in terms of academic and skills achievements than the qualification descriptors of the QAA. In practical terms, if the purpose for descriptors is to act as a guide for writing or assessing the level of learning outcomes, the greater detail in the SEEC descriptors is very significant.

The analysis of the differences between the descriptors below aims mainly to pick out the points of difference which might imply different expectations of learners at the same level in the two sets of descriptors. Other than noting general themes, comment is not made on areas in which the descriptors concur. Because of their orientation toward employers, the qualification descriptors make references to the learner's potential performance in employment, but generally such statements will apply also to the performance of learners who are progressing to a higher level in education.

SEEC level 1/QAA Certificate level (C)

Both sets of descriptors indicate that learners will be proficient at working with basic concepts in their subject areas. The principal difference between the two sets of descriptors is in the reference in the SEEC descriptors to the relative level of guidance provided for learner performance, and correspondingly the degree of autonomy expected and the relative predictability of the subject material with which learners work. References to these general areas of functioning of learners, supervision of learning and the nature of subject matter are generally absent in the QAA descriptors.

It is somewhat difficult to ascertain the notion of level of performance from the QAA qualification descriptors at this level as they do not use concepts such as those of relative guidance or autonomy in the manner of the SEEC descriptors. In general terms, qualification descriptors might be considered to cover a broader range of achievement than the SEEC descriptors, indicating higher achievement than the latter.

SEEC level 2/QAA Intermediate level (I)

Both sets of descriptors describe the learner as gaining flexibility and ability to cope with a broader range of subject matter in more complex contexts, using the main techniques of the discipline. Both sets of descriptors imply the attainment of a better-substantiated understanding of the nature of the subject or the discipline. Generally the SEEC descriptors at this level imply an expectation of increasing autonomy in the learner and an ability to work with material which is less predictable.

The QAA descriptors include references to critical evaluation and critical analysis, which are terms evident in the SEEC descriptors only at level HE3. The QAA descriptors also indicate expectation of a greater proficiency in learners for the communication of information (within and beyond the discipline) in the form of argument and analysis.

For the several reasons indicated above, the QAA qualification descriptors seem to imply the expectation of a higher level of achievement than the SEEC descriptors.

SEEC level 3/QAA Honours level (H)

Learners are expected to be in command of a broad range of knowledge in their subject, with detailed knowledge in some areas. Both sets of descriptors indicate an expectation that learners will have an understanding of the nature of knowledge and independently be able to present and work with it in relatively sophisticated manners that are appropriate to a given context. They are expected to be self-critical and to manage their own learning effectively, and be able critically to review other material. The descriptors both imply that the learner can function in a complex and unpredictable context.

In terms of apparent level differences between the descriptors, QAA descriptors describe learners as working sometimes at the 'forefront' of their discipline. SEEC descriptors place the notion of working with advanced levels of a discipline at Master's level, and working 'at the current limits of theoretical and / or research knowledge' at the level of taught doctorate. There is a greater emphasis on a research orientation for learning in the qualification descriptors at level HE3, with learners using original data or research information.

There are some aspects of the QAA level H descriptors that seem, if anything, to imply a lower level of functioning than the previous level. For example, at level I, learners 'will typically be able to effectively communicate information, arguments, and analysis in a variety of forms to specialist and non-specialist audiences'. At level H, they 'will be able to communicate information, ideas, problems and solutions to both specialist and non-specialist audiences'.

At level 3/level H, perhaps because we are more accustomed to discussing achievement in student learning, the overall pictures of level implied by the two sets of descriptors seem to concur even if they emerge from the description of sometimes differing qualities.

Postgraduate levels: SEEC/QAA descriptors at SEEC Master's and taught doctorate and QAA M and D

In the postgraduate levels, work has been done on the SEEC descriptors in order to align their wording more closely with that of the QAA descriptors as a matter of convenience for the users. For this reason, only a few general comments are made. There is anyway less likelihood of conflict between the two sets of descriptors at postgraduate levels, since qualifications tend to be more stable in terms of credit volume.

At Master's level/level M both sets of descriptors imply that the learner will be relatively autonomous and proficient in using the tools of the discipline for investigation and inquiry. She will be able critically to evaluate research and scholarship in the discipline, using this understanding to solve methodological problems.

At the level of the taught doctorate/level D, there is a difference in the focus of the descriptors. The SEEC descriptors attempt only to describe the level of learning that is derived from 'taught' or managed learning courses that are run at this level. The qualification descriptors focus on research ability and on the learning that emerges as a result of research. The difference is appropriate since credit is normally accorded only to taught/managed learning and not to research. Despite the different focuses, both sets of descriptors imply that the learner is functioning at the forefront of areas of her discipline; is autonomous, can be innovative, understands the complexities of the discipline and can manage unpredictable situations and the difficulties that others may experience in the field.

It is worth remembering at this level that very often the learning/teaching element of taught doctorates is, in fact, located at Master's level and not at taught doctorate level.

Conclusion

In this exercise it is important not to become too caught up in detail in looking at the relative levels implied by sets of descriptors. As we have said before, level descriptors are using very blunt instruments: words with slippery meanings that are used to fashion important but equally slippery statements about student learning. Both sets of descriptors represent attempts to describe something better than we have managed to describe it before.

In terms of the comparison between SEEC credit levels and qualification levels, there is perhaps even a surprisingly close match of level implied by the two systems. In practical terms this can mean that an institution could use either system or both systems, recognizing their approximate parity, and also recognizing that theoretically they may be referring to slightly different structures (elements of a programme or whole qualifications).

Appendix 4 An exercise to facilitate development of 'depth' assessment criteria in reflective writing

Introduction

The rationale for the development and use of this exercise is described in Chapter 8. There follow three accounts of an experience of 22 year-old Marianne who is in her first job after graduating. At the end of the three accounts some suggestions are provided as to why the accounts can be seen as representing different levels of reflection. From these suggestions it would be possible to develop assessment criteria for the quality of depth in reflective writing. The material would also provide a means of indicating to students what might be meant by depth in reflective writing.

The presentation

1.00

I had to take an agenda item to the weekly team meeting in my third week of working at PIGG plc. I had to talk about the project that I am on (creating a new database for the management information system). I had done a presentation before and then I relied on my acting skills. Despite the acting, I spent quite a bit of time preparing it in the way that I have seen others make similar presentations.

The presentation at the last team meeting, given by my colleague, went well. She used PowerPoint and I decided to use it. I decided that a good presentation comes from good planning and having all the figures that anyone might request, so I spent a long time in the preparation and I went in feeling confident.

However, I became nervous when I realized they were all waiting for me to speak, and my nerves made my voice wobble. I did not know how to stop it. Early on, I noticed that people seemed not to understand what I was saying despite the PowerPoint. Using PowerPoint meant that people received my presentation both through what I was saying and what I had prepared on the slides. In a way that meant they got it twice, but I noticed that Mrs Shaw (my boss) repeated bits of what I had said several times and once or twice answered questions for me. This made me feel uncomfortable. I felt it was quite patronizing and I was upset. Later my colleagues said that she always does it. I was disappointed that my presentation did not seem to have gone well.

I thought about the presentation for several days and then talked with Mrs Shaw about the presentation (there was no one else). She gave me a list of points for improvement next time. They included:

- putting less on PowerPoint;
- talking more slowly;
- calming myself down in some way.

I also have to write down the figures in a different way so that they can be understood better. She suggested that I should do a presentation to several of the team sometime next week so that I can improve my performance.

2.00

I had to take an agenda item to the weekly team meeting in my third week of working at PIGG plc. I had to talk about the project that I am on. I am creating a new database for the management information system. I had given a presentation before and that time I relied on my acting skills. I did realize that there were considerable differences between then and now, particularly in the situation (it was only fellow students and my tutor before). I was confident but I did spend quite a bit of time preparing. Because everyone else here uses PowerPoint, I felt I had better use it, although I realized that it was not for the best reasons. I also prepared lots of figures so that I could answer questions. I thought, at that stage, that any questions would involve requests for data. When I think back on the preparation that I did, I realize that I was desperately trying to prove that I could make a presentation as well as my colleague, who did the last one. I wanted to impress everyone. I had not realized there was so much to learn about presenting, and how much I needed to know about PowerPoint to use it properly.

When I set up the presentation in the meeting I tried to be calm but it did not work out. Early on the PowerPoint went wrong and I began to panic. Trying to pretend that I was cool and confident made the situation worse because I did not admit my difficulties and ask for help. The more I spoke, the more my voice went wobbly. I realized, from the kinds of questions that the others asked, that they did not understand what I was saying. They were asking for clarification, not the figures. I felt worse when Mrs Shaw, my boss, started to answer questions for me. I felt flustered and even less able to cope.

As a result of this poor presentation, my self esteem is low at work now. I had thought I was doing all right in the company. After a few days, I went to see Mrs Shaw and we talked it over. I still feel that her interventions did not help me. Interestingly several of my colleagues commented that she always does that. It was probably her behaviour, more than anything else, that damaged my poise. Partly through talking over the presentation and the things that went wrong (but not, of course, her interventions), I can see several areas that I could get better. I need to know more about using PowerPoint, and to practise with it. I recognize, also, that my old acting skills might have given me initial confidence, but I needed more than a clear voice, especially when I lost my way with PowerPoint. Relying on a mass of figures was not right either. It was not figures they wanted. In retrospect, I could have put the figures on a handout. I am hoping to have a chance to try with another presentation, practising with some of the team.

3.00

I am writing this back in my office. It all happened 2 days ago.

Three weeks after I started at PIGG plc had to take an agenda item to the team meeting. I was required to report on my progress in the project on which I am working. I am developing a new database for the management information system of the company. I was immediately worried. I was scared about not saying the right things and not being able to answer questions properly. I did a presentation in my course at university and felt the same about it initially. I was thinking then, like this time, that I could use my acting skills. Both times that was helpful in maintaining my confidence at first, at least, although the fact that I was all right last time through the whole presentation may not have helped me this time!

I decided to use PowerPoint. I was not very easy about its use because I have seen it go wrong so often. However, I have not seen anyone else give a presentation here without using it, and learning to use PowerPoint would be valuable. I was not sure, when it came to the session, whether I really knew enough about running PowerPoint. (How do you know when you know enough about something? Dummy runs, I suppose, but I couldn't get the laptop when I wanted it.)

When it came to the presentation, I really wanted to do it well – as well as the presentations were done the week before. Maybe I wanted too much to do well. Previous presentations have been interesting, informative and clear, and I thought the handouts from them were good (I noticed that the best gave enough but not too much information).

In the event, the session was a disaster. It has left me feeling uncomfortable in my work, and I even worry about it at home. I need to think about why a simple presentation could have such an effect on me. The PowerPoint went wrong (I think I clicked on the wrong thing). My efforts to be calm and 'cool' failed and my voice went wobbly – that was, anyway, how it felt to me. My colleague actually said afterwards that I looked quite calm despite what I was feeling (I am not sure whether she meant it or was trying to help me). When I think back to that moment, if I had thought that I still looked calm (despite what I felt), I could have regained the situation. As it was, it went from bad to worse and I know that my state became obvious because Mrs Shaw, my boss, began to answer the questions that people were asking for me.

I am thinking about the awful presentation again – it was this time last week. I am reading what I wrote earlier about it. Now I return to it, I do have a slightly different perspective. I think that it was not as bad as it felt at the time. Several of my colleagues told me afterwards that Mrs Shaw always steps in to answer questions like that, and they commented that I handled her intrusion well. That is interesting. I need to do some thinking about how to act next time to prevent this interruption from happening or to deal with the situation when she starts.* I might look in the library for that book on assertiveness.

I have talked to Mrs Shaw now too. I notice that my confidence in her is not all that great while I am still feeling a bit cross. However, I am feeling more positive generally and I can begin to analyse what I could do better in the presentation. It is interesting to see the change in my attitude after a week. I need to think from the beginning about the process of giving a good presentation. I am not sure how helpful was my reliance on my acting skills.* Acting helped my voice to be stronger and better paced, but I was trying to put over not someone else's lines but my own, and I needed to be able to discuss matters in greater depth rather than just give the line.*

I probably will use PowerPoint again. I have had a look in the manual and it suggests that you treat it as a tool, not let it dominate, and not use it as a means of presenting itself. That is what I think I was doing. I need not only to know how to use it, but to feel sufficiently confident in its use that I can retrieve the situation when things go wrong. That means understanding more than just the sequence of actions.*

As I am writing this, I am noticing how useful it is to go back over things I have written about before. I seem to be able to see the situation differently. The first time I wrote this, I felt that the presentation was dreadful and that I could not have done it differently. Then later I realized that there were things I did not know at the time (eg about Mrs Shaw and her habit of interrupting). I also recognize some of the areas in which I went wrong. At the time I could not see that. It was as if my low self esteem got in the way. Knowing where I went wrong and admitting the errors to myself gives me a chance to improve next time – and perhaps to help Mrs Shaw to improve in her behaviour towards us!

* I have asterisked the points that I need to address in order to improve.

Features of the accounts that are indicative of different levels of reflection

1.00

This account is descriptive and it contains little reflection.

- The account describes what happened, sometimes mentioning past experiences, sometimes anticipating the future, but all in the context of an account of the event.

- There are some references to Marianne's emotional reactions, but she has not explored how the reactions relate to her behaviour.
- Ideas are taken on without questioning them or considering them in depth.
- The account is written only from Marianne's point of view.
- External information is mentioned but its impact on behaviour is not subject to consideration.
- Generally one point is made at a time and ideas are not linked.

2.00

An account showing evidence of some reflection.

- There is description of the event, but where there are external ideas or information, the material is subjected to consideration and deliberation.
- The account shows some analysis.
- There is recognition of the worth of exploring motives for behaviour
- There is willingness to be critical of action.
- Relevant and helpful detail is explored where it has value.
- There is recognition of the overall effect of the event on self: in other words, there is some 'standing back' from the event.
- The account is written at one point in time. It does not, therefore, demonstrate the recognition that views can change with time and more reflection. In other words, the account does not indicate a recognition that frames of reference affect the manner in which we reflect at a given time.

3.00

This account shows quite deep reflection, and it does incorporate a recognition that the frame of reference with which an event is viewed can change.

- Self questioning is evident (an 'internal dialogue' is set up at times) deliberating between different views of her own behaviour (different views of her own and others).

- Marianne takes into account the views and motives of others and considers these against her own.
- She recognizes how prior experience and thoughts (her own and other's) interact with the production of her own behaviour.
- There is clear evidence of standing back from an event.
- She helps herself to learn from the experience by splitting off the reflective processes from the points she wants to learn (by asterisk system).
- There is recognition that the personal frame of reference can change according to the emotional state in which it is written, the acquisition of new information, the review of ideas and the effect of time passing.

Glossary

APL or APEL	accreditation of prior learning or of prior experiential learning
APU	Anglia Polytechnic University
CATS	credit accumulation and transfer systems
CNAA	Council for National Academic Awards
DfEE	Department of Education and Employment
EWNI	shorthand for England, Wales and Northern Ireland (in NQF connection)
HECIW	Higher Education Credit Initiative Wales
InCCA	Inter-consortium Credit Agreement
LTSN	Learning and Teaching Subject Network
NCIHE	National Council of Inquiry into Higher Education
NHSTD	National Health Service Training Directorate
NICATS	Northern Ireland Credit Accumulation and Transfer System
NVQ	National Vocational Qualifications
QAA	Quality Assurance Agency
QCA	Qualifications and Curriculum Agency
QF	National Qualifications Framework
SEDA	Staff and Educational Development Association
SEEC	Southern England Consortium for Credit Accumulation and Transfer
SRHE	Society for Research into Higher Education
UCE	University of Central England
UCoSDA	University and Colleges Staff Development Association
UEL	University of East London
UfI	University for Industry

References

Allan, J (1996) Learning outcomes in higher education, *Studies in Higher Education*, **21**(1), pp 93–108

Angelo, T and Cross, K (1990) *Classroom Assessment Techniques*, Jossey-Bass, San Francisco, California

Belenky, M, Clinchy, B, Goldberger, R and Tarule, J (1986) *Women's Ways of Knowing*, Basic Books, New York

Bement, M and Lyons, F (1994) Skills and attainment matrices, Partnerships Office, University of Portsmouth

Bloom, B (1956) *Taxonomy of Educational Objectives: The cognitive domain*, David McKay, New York

Boud, D (1995) *Enhancing Learning Through Self Assessment*, Kogan Page, London

Boud, D and Falchikov, N (1989) Quantitative studies of student self assessment in higher education: a critical analysis of findings, *Higher Education*, **18**(5), pp 529–49

Broadfoot, P (2000) Assessment and intuition, in *The Intuitive Practitioner*, ed T Atkinson and G Claxton, Open University Press, Buckingham

Brown, S and Dove, P (1991) *Peer and Self Assessment*, Standing Conference on Educational Development (SCED), Birmingham

Brown, S and Glasner, A (1999) *Assessment Matters in Higher Education*, Society for Research into Higher Education (SRHE)/Open University Press, Buckingham

Brown, S and Knight, P (1994) *Assessing Learners in Higher Education*, Kogan Page, London

CNAA (1991) *Handbook*, Council for National Academic Awards, London

D'Andrea, V (1999) Organising teaching and learning, outcomes-based planning, in *A Handbook on Teaching and Learning in Higher Education*, ed H Fry, S Ketteridge and S Marshall, Kogan Page, London

Dillon, C and Hodgkinson, L (2000) Programme specification in a flexible, multidisciplinary environment, *Quality Assurance in Education*, **8**(4), pp 203–10

Eisner, E (1991) Forms of understanding and the future of education, *Educational Researcher*, **22**, pp 5–11

Entwistle, N and Entwistle, A (1992) Experience of understanding in revising for degree examinations, *Learning and Instruction*, **2**, pp 1–22

Fulwiler, T (1987) *The Journal Book*, Heinemann, Portsmouth, New Hampshire

George, J and Cowan, J (1999) *A Handbook of Techniques for Formative Evaluation*, Kogan Page, London

Gibbs, G (1995) *Assessing Student-Centred Courses*, Oxford Centre for Staff Development, Oxford Brookes University, Oxford

Gosling, D and Moon, J (2001) *How to Use Learning Outcomes and Assessment Criteria*, SEEC, University of East London, London

Hatton, N and Smith, D (1995) Reflection in teacher education: towards definition and implementation, *Teaching and Teacher Education*, **11**(1), pp 33–49

HECIW (1996) *Higher Education Credit Framework Handbook*, Wales Access Unit, Cardiff

Hounsell, D, McCullough, M and Scott, M (1996) *Changing Assessment Practices in Scottish Higher Education (ASSHE Inventory)* Edinburgh, Napier Universities, UCoSDA

InCCA (1998) *A Common Framework for Learning*, DfEE, London

Jackson, N (1999) *Continuing Development Awards Framework: Draft design principles for application in higher education*, University for Industry, Sheffield

Jackson, N (2000) Guest editor, 'Programme specification', theme of *Quality Assurance in Education*, **8**(4)

Johnson, R and Walsh, A (2000) *Credit Practice: A comparative approach 1994–1999*, SEEC, London

Jordan, S (1999) Self-assessment and peer-assessment, in *Assessment Matters in Higher Education*, ed S Brown and A Glasner, SRHE/Open University Press, Buckingham

King, P and Kitchener, K (1994) *Developing Reflective Judgement*, Jossey-Bass, San Francisco, California

Kneale, P (1997) The rise of the 'strategic' student; how can we adapt to cope?, in *Facing up to Radical Changes in Universities and Colleges*, ed M Armstrong, G Thompson and S Brown, SEDA/Kogan Page, London

Kolb, D (1984) *Experiential Learning as the Science of Learning and Development*, Prentice-Hall, Englewood Cliffs, New Jersey

Mager, R (1975) *Preparing Instructional Objectives*, Pitman Learning, Belmont, California

Marton, F, Hounsell, D and Entwistle, N (1997) *The Experience of Learning*, Scottish Academic Press, Edinburgh

Methven, P (1994) *Levels Descriptors: A guide for advisory groups and writers*, New Zealand Qualifications Authority

Moon, J (1975) Some thoughts on study skills, *Reading*, **10**, pp 24–34

Moon, J (1995a) *Development of Foundation Courses in Health Promotion*, prepared for the Health Education Authority, Health Education Board for Scotland, Health Promotion Wales and Health Promotion Authority for Northern Ireland, Cardiff

Moon, J (1995b) *Levels in Higher Education*, UCoSDA briefing paper 27, December

Moon, J (1995c) *Credit in Higher Education: The implications for staff development*, UCoSDA briefing paper 26, December

Moon, J (1999a) *Reflection in Learning and Professional Development*, Kogan Page, London

Moon, J (1999b) *Learning Journals: A handbook for academics, students and professional development*, Kogan Page, London

Moon, J (1999c) Describing higher education: some conflicts and conclusions, in *Benchmarking and Threshold Standards in Higher Education*, ed H Smith, M Armstrong and S Brown, SEDA/Kogan Page, London

Moon, J (2000) Reflection: an intellectual process or an academic mind-game?, for SEDA Mini-conference on Reflection, October

Moon, J (2001a) Comparison of the QAA qualification level descriptors and the SEEC credit level descriptors, *SEEC News*, Summer, University of East London, London

Moon, J (2001b) *Short Courses and Workshops: Improving the impact of learning and professional development*, Kogan Page, London, chapter 1

Moon, J (2001c, in preparation) Reflection in higher education learning, paper for Learning and Teaching Subject Network Web site

Moon, J and England, P (1994) Professional development: foundation for health promotion, *Health Education Journal*, **53**, pp 100–106

NCIHE (1997) *Higher Education in the Learning Society*, report of the National Committee of Inquiry into Higher Education chaired by Sir Ron Dearing, NCIHE/97/850, HMSO, London

NHSTD (1994) *Supporting Health Pickup for CATS Credits*, A handbook for advisors and co-ordinators, NHSTD, Bristol

NICATS (1998) *A Credit Framework as a Vehicle for Lifelong Learning*, Northern Ireland Credit Accumulation and Transfer System, Northern Ireland

Otter, S (1992) *Learning Outcomes in Higher Education*, report for Universities Association for Continuing Education

Perry, W (1970) *Forms of Intellectual and Academic Developments in the College Years*, Holt, Rinehart and Winston, New York

QAA (2000a) *Guidelines for Preparing Programme Specifications*, QAA, Gloucester

QAA (2000b) *The National Qualifications Framework for England, Wales and Northern Ireland: A position paper*, QAA, Gloucester, July

QAA (2000c) *Handbook for Academic Review*, QAA, Gloucester

QAA (2000d) *Final Report of the Advisory Group on Multidisciplinary and Modular Programmes*, QAA, Gloucester

QAA (2001a) *A Framework for Higher Education Qualifications in England, Wales and Northern Ireland*, QAA, Gloucester

QAA (2001b) *The Framework of Qualifications of Higher Education Institutions in Scotland*, QAA, Gloucester

QAA (www) QAA Web site. This includes all the documents published by the QAA. This reference is given for the subject benchmark statements in particular: www.QAA.ac.uk

QCA (www) NVQ level statements http://www.qca.org.uk/nq/subjects/qlnvq7.asp

Race, P (1991) Self and peer assessment, in *Peer and Self Assessment*, ed S Brown and P Dove, SCED, Birmingham

Richards, P (1992) Internal discussion paper for CATS/APL Group, University of Central England, Birmingham

Robertson, D (1994) *Choosing to Change*, report prepared for HEQC CAT Development Project, London

SEEC (1996) *Credit Guidelines, Models and Protocols*, SEEC, University of East London, London

SEEC (1996a) *Guidelines for Credit and General Credit Rating*, SEEC, University of East London, London

Stones, E and Anderson, D (1972) *Educational Objectives and the Teaching of Educational Psychology*, Methuen, London

Trigwell, K and Prosser, M (1999) *Understanding Learning and Teaching*, SRHE /Open University Press, Buckingham

Watton, P, Collings, J and Moon, J (2002, in preparation) SEDA paper on work experience (no title yet), SEDA, Birmingham

Winter, R (1993) *The Problem of Educational Levels: Conceptualising a framework for credit accumulation and transfer*, David McKay, New York

Winter, R (1994) Identifying 'progression' through 'transferable learning skills'?, paper commissioned for the Further Education Unit, London

Winter, R (1994a) The problem of educational levels, part 11: a new framework for credit accumulation and transfer, *Journal of Further and Higher Education*, **18**(1)

Index

Notes:

See the glossary for the interpretation of initials / acromyms. Chapter 10 (the summary of the book) has its own page reference system. It is not indexed below)